Individualists Who Co-operate

Individualists Who Co-operate:

Education and welfare reform befitting a free people

David G. Green

Civitas: Institute for the Study of Civil Society
London
Registered Charity No. 1085494

First Published January 2009

© Civitas 2009
77 Great Peter Street
London SW1P 2EZ
Civitas is a registered charity (no. 1085494)
and a company limited by guarantee, registered in
England and Wales (no. 04023541)

email: books@civitas.org.uk

ISBN 978-1-906837-02-0

Typeset by
Civitas

Printed in Great Britain by
The Cromwell Press
Trowbridge, Wiltshire

Contents

Author

David G. Green is the Director of Civitas. His books include *The New Right: The Counter Revolution in Political, Economic and Social Thought*, Wheatsheaf, 1987; *Reinventing Civil Society*, IEA, 1993; *Community Without Politics: A Market Approach to Welfare Reform*, IEA 1996; *Benefit Dependency: How Welfare Undermines Independence*, IEA, 1999; *Delay, Denial and Dilution*, IEA, 1999 (with Laura Casper); *Stakeholder Health Insurance*, Civitas, 2000; *Health Care in France and Germany: Lessons for the UK*, Civitas 2001 (with Ben Irvine); *Crime and Civil Society*, Civitas 2005 (with Emma Grove and Nadia Martin); *We're (Nearly) All Victims Now*, Civitas 2006. He wrote the chapter on 'The Neo-Liberal Perspective' in Blackwell's *The Student's Companion to Social Policy*, (2nd edn) 2003.

He writes occasionally for newspapers, including in recent years pieces in *The Times* and *The Sunday Times* (on race, education, welfare, the NHS and crime), the *Sunday Telegraph* (on crime, education and victim culture) and the *Daily Telegraph* (on crime, immigration, education and welfare reform).

Preface

The economic downturn has forced us to question some of the unchallenged assumptions of our time. In particular we need to ask whether our welfare system is worthy of the challenges it now faces.

People who work hard and pay their taxes are the backbone of society. When political parties praise 'hard-working families', as they all now do, they acknowledge this basic reality. However, the continued willingness of hard-working people to go on paying taxes depends on an implicit contract between them and the recipients of welfare benefits. There must be reciprocity.

Most taxpayers know that they are paying for their own upkeep and that of other people less fortunate than them. And they are fully aware that they are also paying for public services like health and education for other people as well as themselves. These obligations have been accepted willingly. However, it has been obvious for a while that some people receiving benefits could work but choose not to. And it has also become apparent that health and education services are not as good as they could be. It is generally acknowledged that the huge spending on the NHS since 1997 has not produced improvements proportionate to the investment, and in education even the Government is dissatisfied with standards.

The vast majority of people gladly pay into a common fund to ensure that everyone receives good health care and education. But this determination to guarantee access for everyone has been confused with a desire for absolute political control. And the result has been to suppress the most effective method of maintaining high standards—competition.

We remain a kindly people unwilling to permit the least well off to go without, but perhaps there are other ways of

achieving the same ideal without the public sector monopolies in health and education that appear to drag down
standards. This book focuses on welfare and education (the
NHS must await another publication). I argue that we could
discharge our obligation to the least fortunate members of
society more effectively without destroying the element of
competition that is vital to maintaining high standards for us
all.

If the only way to provide guarantees for the least
fortunate Britons inevitably involved lower standards for the
others, there might still be a majority in favour of the status
quo. But no such claim holds water. Indeed, in education it
is children from poor backgrounds who are now being failed
by state monopoly. The majority of hard-working taxpayers
need to be granted independence from state control for the
sake of their least fortunate neighbours, not in spite of them.

Is such a change a realistic possibility? One of the
fractures that can weaken a society is between the ruling
elite and the rank and file, but we may be going through a
time when the fallacious beliefs of the elite are being
compelled to adjust to the inescapable realities experienced
by everyone else. The main political parties are keen to insist
that we can't have rights without duties and that we must
take responsibility for our own affairs. They appear to
recognise that the grand designs of party manifestos can't be
fulfilled without the willing co-operation of ordinary people.
Much of what tends to be promised has never been within
the gift of government but rather relies on individual
decisions about lifestyle or behaviour. Health outcomes, for
example, depend a good deal on personal decisions about
smoking, drinking and exercise, and educational attainment
is not purely a function of classroom teaching practices but is
heavily influenced by parents. In a speech in September 2007
Gordon Brown recognised that 'we have not done enough in

the last ten years to emphasise that in return for the rights we all have, there are responsibilities we all owe.' And David Cameron has even gone so far as to say that people should stop making excuses for unwanted outcomes like being overweight. He ridiculed people who spoke about being 'at risk of obesity' as if outside forces were at work, when the remedy lay in their own hands.

This is all a far cry from the era in which holding anyone responsible for anything was 'blaming the victim', a sure sign of a callous person out for himself. But if personal responsibility is the new watchword, what does it imply for public policy reform? This short book is my attempt to suggest what it *should* mean. Above all, we need to give our backing to people who by working hard and paying taxes make a kindly society a realistic possibility.

This publication is partly an extended version of an essay published in the January 2007 edition of *Civitas Review* and takes account of comments and criticisms voiced at the time. I am particularly grateful to Norman Dennis, Alasdair Palmer, Robert Whelan, Bob Rowthorn, Peter Saunders, Claire Daley, Catherine Green and Justin Shaw for their comments.

David G. Green

Summary

Introduction and Chapter 2

1. Earned independence is being undermined. If you go out to work and earn enough to keep yourself and to pay for health, education and welfare for less fortunate people—willingly—you should not be prevented from choosing health and education services that meet your own needs best, especially when there is no cost to anyone else.

2. Public services: there is more than one way of ensuring that poverty is never a barrier to good health care and education. The ideal of social solidarity has been achieved in several other countries without government monopolies that suppress beneficial competition.

3. Welfare: the majority of the British people are more than happy to pay taxes to provide for other people in genuine need. And they are more than happy to give the benefit of the doubt to borderline cases. We are a generous people. But it is only right that people who are able to work should take a job if one is available.

4. The theory that our public services were poor quality mainly because of under-spending has been tested to destruction since 1997 by huge increases in expenditure on health, education and welfare. Continued dissatisfaction with public services is not due to incompetent political leaders nor to an exhausted government. It is because we have reached the limits of effective political action.

5. The distinctive characteristic of political action is not pursuit of the common good but pursuit of the aims of government armed with concentrated and exclusive power. This power has been used partly for the public

good, but also to serve producer interests and to advance the interests of the ruling party.

6. We urgently need to re-frame the constitutional settlement that defines the relationship between the state and the individual in civil society. The state should be confined to the legitimate tasks that are within its competence, thus allowing greater scope for private enterprise and social entrepreneurs to supply public services more effectively.

7. It is not enough for the government merely to 'get out of the way'. The challenge is to create a sphere of public liberty in which private individuals can pursue the common good in co-operation with one another. The size of this sphere of private action for the public good is the measure of a good society.

8. The English heritage of liberty is based on the idea of an independent community of people conceived as a kind of membership association that had founded a system of self-government to protect personal security, encourage open and democratic government, and provide for individual liberty under the law.

9. Open and representative government is accomplished, not through majoritarian democracy, which implies enforcing fixed opinions, but by encouraging deliberative democracy—listening and reflecting before deciding.

10. A defence of the tradition of liberty must be more than a scheme for reducing the scope of government. It must also provide a strategy for private action to supersede failed collectivism.

11. Historically liberty was the ideal of those who wanted to free human talent and energy for higher purposes in

every walk of life. The point of life was not to pass the time with as little inconvenience and as much personal pleasure as possible. It was to do your bit to enhance the society to which you belonged, perhaps modestly by improving conditions in your own town or village, or if you were fortunate enough to have a special talent, to add to the advance of human civilisation in your chosen sphere.

Chapter 3

1. We have a major problem of welfare dependency whether measured by the proportion of the population receiving benefits or the cost as a proportion of GDP. In 1949/50 all social security benefits cost 4.7 per cent of GDP; by 1969/70 it had gone up to 7.1 per cent. In 2006/07 social protection expenditure was 13.4 per cent of GDP.

2. In 2008/09 45 per cent of families in the UK received more in cash benefits and tax credits (all cash benefits, tax credits, SERPS and the state second pension) than they paid in personal taxes (income tax, national insurance and council tax). In 1979 it was 35 per cent.

3. The majority of families still have private earnings that exceed net state benefits (benefits and tax credits less taxes and NI). The proportion has fluctuated over time: in 2008/09 73 per cent had private income in excess of net state benefits. In 1979 it had been 75 per cent before falling to 69 per cent in 1996/97.

4. The working tax credit discourages full-time work by subsidising individuals who work as few as 16 hours a week when poverty is best avoided by full-time work; and it imposes a penalty on living as a couple, which is

the most effective way of avoiding poverty when children are involved.

5. To be in poverty is not just to lack money. The cash shortfall is the result of other problems and it can only be dealt with effectively by discovering what those problems are and solving them. Giving people money gives them less reason to solve their problems for themselves. In those cases where the problem can *only* be solved by them, then their dependency increases. Not all problems can be solved by the individual concerned. This is obviously true of people who become too ill or disabled to work. But there are many problems that can't be solved without the enthusiastic effort of the individual concerned.

6. Because of the ambiguities and inconsistencies in official policy-making we need to re-state fundamental principles. As the opening premise, we should define ourselves as a kind of membership association that will never allow a member to suffer material hardship.

7. Such a guarantee can only be based on reciprocity, which means that we must define the reasonable expectations we can have of each other. With due allowance for factors beyond individual control, we can reasonably expect that everyone capable of work will try to be self-sufficient by working, select an economically and socially viable family structure, provide for contingencies like unexpected inability to work or the early death of the breadwinner, and predictable lifecycle events like having children and getting older.

8. Policies of equalisation have led to the redistribution of income from a starting point of 15:1 to 4:1 when comparing the top 20 per cent of earners with the

lowest 20 per cent. One of the more remarkable consequences of this massive equalisation is the extent to which many people in the middle of the income distribution and above pay personally for the cash and other benefits they receive from the government. How sensible is it for the government to take money from us and give it back as cash or services (after deducting its own costs)? Would it be more beneficial for people to make their own arrangements with their own money?

9. On average the original income (wages, salaries, interest and dividends) of the sixth decile in 2006/07 was £25,104. Each household received from the government average cash benefits of £4,363, but also paid direct taxes (income tax, national insurance and council tax) of £5,620. Each household also paid average indirect taxes (such as VAT and duties on alcohol, petrol and tobacco) of £4,742 and also received state services (benefits in kind such as the NHS and education) valued at £6,140. In total, each household paid average taxes of £10,362 and received state benefits in cash or kind of £10,503. The average final income, after taking into account churning, was £25,245 — £141 more than their market income.

10. Policy recommendations:

   • Working tax credit should be abolished and replaced by a wage top-up that is only paid to individuals who have worked a 35-hour week for 47 weeks of the year. The guiding principle should be, not that 'no one should ever be poor', but that 'no one who *works hard* should be poor'.

   • Let people keep their own earnings and take responsibility for their own services.

- Marriage should be encouraged and the tax system made more flexible to allow couples to divide the responsibility for caring and earning as they believe best. Income splitting should be introduced, not only for children but also for elderly parents to encourage family support.

- Compulsory saving for old age should be reduced to the minimum. Individuals should be required only to build up a fund equivalent to the income support level and to be otherwise free to make their own arrangements.

- Family trust funds should be encouraged based on the tax treatment of ISAs, namely that contributions are made with after-tax income but subject to no further tax while earning interest or after withdrawal.

- Restore provision against insurable contingencies, like ill health or certainties like death, to the independent sector.

Chapter 4

1. State education provision has for many years failed the least fortunate members of society. The worst performing schools are concentrated in localities where poverty is worst. State education has failed to achieve its primary aim of preventing early disadvantage from acting as a break on achievement throughout adulthood.

2. It has failed because of the inherent flaws in the political process, namely over-concentration of power, the side-effects of political struggle including the manipulation of official information for party advantage, and the suppression of social entrepreneurs.

3. School choice within the state system is pseudo-choice. For effective choice parents should have effective spending power and it should be easy to establish new schools.

4. The vital change we need today is to end public-sector monopoly to open the way for inventive newcomers. The mistake we made during the twentieth century was to believe that the state was the best agency for discharging the common good. We have now learnt that it might not be. The reality is that the power of the state, initially conceded to fill gaps in private provision and to fulfil shared public goals, has been captured by groups with other purposes.

5. The chief defence of competition is that, by ending monopoly, it will raise standards in all schools that face competitive comparison with rivals. Competition has the potential to lift standards in all schools, private and state, as the Wisconsin study revealed. If we allow people to pay less tax and spend their earnings on services everyone will benefit.

6. We need a new settlement that respects earned independence. Currently many people have gone out to work and earned an income sufficient to pay for health and education only to find heavy taxation prevents them from securing better services. People on middle incomes are being taxed by an amount almost identical to the benefits they receive.

7. Policy recommendations:

   • The Government should de-regulate the supply side to encourage the founding of new schools.

   • The Government should transfer state schools to the independent sector.

- A voucher scheme should be introduced. A school able to attract a minimum number of pupils (perhaps 50) should have a right to receive voucher finance.

- Existing private schools should be permitted to receive voucher finance.

- The restoration of spending power would be more effectively restored through a tax allowance, but a voucher scheme would be a significant step forward.

8. It is surely highly anomalous that objections are rarely raised to parents spending freely on frivolous self-indulgences, while spending freely on their child's education is the subject of constant rebuke. The primary obligation of the nation as a membership association is to ensure that every child has access to a good education, not to discriminate against well-paid parents.

9. The state as a membership association should never suppress the potential achievements of any individual, nor condone jealousy. If some parents wish to spend more than others on their children's education they should be permitted to do so, whether they are spending out of their excess income or scrimping and saving to give their children the best they can afford.

10. It is now well established that the key to the successful functioning of any market is the possibility that new entrants will attract customers from existing providers. For this reason, it would be desirable for neither central government nor local authorities to have the power to run any new schools, and to relinquish control of existing schools. This could be accomplished by means of a phased hand-over to independent educational trusts. Primary schools in particular could be run by

people in each locality, thereby providing a way of harnessing the energy and commitment of public-spirited people everywhere. As Mill pointed out, when the state monopolises everything it drives out opportunities for public service and self-development.

1

Introduction

With a General Election due by May 2010 at the latest, political parties know that there is no time for fundamental changes in public perceptions. To stand any chance, they have got to make themselves attractive to public opinion as it already is. Of course, politicians may misinterpret majority feelings and indulge in wishful thinking, but even allowing for such mistakes party standpoints can tell us a lot about the prevailing consensus.

Three opinions have achieved such widespread acceptance that they are being embraced by all the parties. All favour more 'choice' in health and education; they each claim to champion 'hard-working families'; and all are united in breaking with the one-sided culture of 'rights' in favour of 'rights and responsibilities'.

Gordon Brown, David Cameron and Nick Clegg all accept that the rights of citizenship bring responsibilities. Moreover, not everyone who is poor can blame society or 'the system' for their predicament. The Government likes to use the neutral language of the social sciences to express home truths and has long said that 'worklessness' is a primary cause of poverty. Translated into a practical maxim, it is another way of saying that if you want to escape poverty you should get a full-time job. However, as I will argue in Chapter 3, welfare reform leaves much to be desired.

More choice has long been a slogan of public policy reform. We are in the process of being granted more choice of doctor and school, and even policing is to be made more accountable through localised 'crime maps' and the election of local Crime and Policing Representatives. Giving us all choice and making public officials more accountable implies

1

a society made up of people with an understanding of the issues, the ability to evaluate rival arguments, and an inclination to take personal responsibility for their own affairs. In other words, the new political agenda assumes a free people. However, as I will discuss in Chapter 4, we are a long way from having a genuine choice of school.

All the main parties claim to champion 'hard-working families'. Such families are also thought to be deserving of tax cuts, which implies that people should be allowed to spend their earnings as they believe best. The Liberal Democrats are planning a cut of 4p in the basic rate of income tax, the Tories plan to 'share' the proceeds of growth and Labour has already cut the basic rate to 20p. But, as later chapters will also show, we still have a long way to go before 'hard-working families' genuinely have full responsibility for their own affairs.

The consensus among all parties for many decades has been that our problems are best solved by enacting laws that require stipulated behaviour, or by establishing government agencies to provide services. However, there may be something about government or the political process as such that makes policy failure more likely. Politics invariably rests on the assumption that there is 'one best solution'. We tend to romanticise the democratic state as an institution that reflects the will of the people, but it is primarily the institution in society that is entitled to use compulsion, which in practice means concentrated and exclusive power.

In all three main parties the age-old dispute continues about the limits that should be placed on the power of government. Some voices among the Liberal Democrats — the contributors to the Orange Book, edited by Paul Marshall and David Laws — are calling for a liberalism that reflects valid concerns about over-mighty government.[1]

Blairites in the Labour party have continuing doubts about producer-dominated public services and people who call themselves 'left-liberals' ought to find much to agree with in this book. Nick Cohen has recently written *What's Left?*, sub-titled 'how liberals lost their way', and Andrew Anthony has constructed a powerful defence of left-liberalism in *The Fallout*.[2] Philip Collins and Richard Reeves have recently called for a revival of the new liberalism in *Prospect* magazine,[3] which under the able editorship of David Goodhart has provided a good home for liberal voices on the left for over a decade, including writers such as Bob Rowthorn, John Lloyd and Paul Ormerod.

The Conservatives have in their midst three potentially supportive groups: enthusiasts for a compassionate conservatism that respects the role of an autonomous civil society; those who champion a new Tory fraternalism that acknowledges that we are 'all in it together' without embracing statism; and advocates of direct democracy. Jesse Norman has ably defended compassionate conservatism following earlier contributions by David Willetts.[4] A new Tory fraternalism has been advocated by Danny Kruger[5] and direct democracy has been championed by Douglas Carswell and Dan Hannan among others.[6]

Where should we be on the continuum that has totalitarianism at one end and liberalism at the other? The Tories who are concerned about the failure of public sector monopolies in health and education are anxious to differentiate themselves from market fundamentalists, but know that calling for a reduced role for the state in health and education is to invite being caricatured as uncaring. Is there an idea that could be embraced by people of good will in all parties who see the dangers of intrusive government but who reject laissez faire? I will argue that the idea of a nation as a membership association—a membership state—provides useful guiding principles.

Is it realistic to propose a strategy in the hope that it might be embraced by any of the leading political parties? Isn't the Labour party particularly unlikely to embrace market liberalism? It is true that political parties all contain diehard supporters of various doctrines and that Labour is the primary home of egalitarian collectivists who want to extend the power of government. However, modern political parties are coalitions of convenience for winning elections and all contain many activists who are pragmatic problem-solvers, which makes them capable of reversing policy commitments once regarded as virtually sacred. Simon Jenkins has convincingly demonstrated the debt owed to Thatcherism by both Blair and Brown.[7] All parties have to reach a view about the real or perceived problems of the day and all need to advocate convincing solutions.

This essay suggests one approach to the role of government that could work. Intellectually it owes a lot to John Stuart Mill, who was one of many thinkers in the late nineteenth century trying to develop liberalism beyond laissez faire whilst remaining recognisably liberal. Since then, we have gone through the age of collectivism, the Thatcherite reaction to it, and New Labour's response. During the 1980s there was a time when laissez faire seemed to have made an unlikely comeback, but it did not sink deep roots beyond a few hard-boiled economists and lifestyle libertarians. We have yet to reach a consensus on the kind of relationship the people of Britain want with their government. The idea of the minimal state is still there, but more as a talking point than a practical option. The idea of limited government (as opposed to totalitarian rule that puts no constraints on what the state might do) is well understood across the spectrum. The present government

4

has revealed a strong desire for a powerful state to provide health care, education and social security among other things, but it fully realises that a market economy to create wealth is unavoidable.

Is there a coherent alternative that better defines the proper roles of government and people? And is it, as I claim, one that could appeal to left liberals in the Labour party, genuine liberals among the Liberal Democrats, and to Conservatives who are not paternalistic? The term I have chosen to describe this alternative is the 'membership state'. It can be contrasted with the minimal state and the provider state.

Before turning to specific reforms, Chapter 2 appraises the guiding principles that have typically been at the core of British liberty.

2

The Guiding Principles
of a Free People

The main liberal concern has always been the abuse of absolute power. Some who shared this concern (like William Godwin in the eighteenth century) opposed all government but liberals advocated *limited* government. Modern liberalism evolved from the middle of the seventeenth century and took more than one form but the common thread has been a search for the best way to harness legitimate compulsion to pursuit of the common good while avoiding the abuse of power or opening the way for a return of autocratic and unlimited rule. From Locke onwards we can conveniently group liberal concerns under three headings: the grounds of legitimate authority, the legitimate ends of government and the legitimate means of pursuing them.

Legitimate authority

Consent: From the time of Locke, liberals thought that the legitimacy of government rested on the consent of the people being governed, and not on the divine right of kings or on the alleged personal superiority (whether due to breeding or education) of rulers.[1] Power was not permanent and unlimited, but temporary and conditional. Consent implied elections to secure peaceful changes of regime, but also an ultimate right of rebellion if there were no possibility of peaceful change.

Legitimate ends

Liberals believed that government should pursue the common good and maintain a sphere of individual freedom.

The common good: Consent also implied that the only legitimate end of government is to serve the common good as opposed to sectional interests. Liberalism has had many enemies and they often attributed views to liberals they did not hold.[2] These claims boil down to three main assertions: liberals favour atomised individualism; liberals ignore the common good; and liberals favour unfettered selfishness or egoism.

Social atomisation is not defended by any mainstream liberal, such as Locke, Hume or Smith. How did the misunderstanding arise? Liberals were critics of the social order of their day, which was aristocratic and hierarchical. For them, in law and politics, people should be treated on their individual merits, not according to their birth. They especially objected to the idea of inherited social superiority. In that sense they were individualists, but their individualism took the form of equality before the law, a social 'invention'. They knew only too well that shared beliefs and institutions were the bedrock of society. Justice, said Adam Smith was 'the main pillar that upholds the whole edifice'.[3] He also thought that people should seek to do right according to conscience: 'That the sense of duty should be the sole principle of our conduct, is nowhere the precept of Christianity', but 'it should be the ruling and the governing one, as philosophy, and as, indeed, common sense, directs'.[4] These were not the words of someone who thought that we are all isolated individuals.

Were liberals indifferent to the common good? Locke repeatedly used the terms 'common good' and 'public good' throughout the *Second Treatise of Government*. It is true that he was suspicious of those who *pretended* to desire the common good, but that was an objection to pretence, not the reality. The early liberals were suspicious of those who wanted to impose religious orthodoxy allegedly for the common good, but they thought that justice and the fruits of peaceful co-existence were genuine public goods, as the passage just quoted from Adam Smith testifies.

Did liberals celebrate selfishness? Again, liberals were very far from celebrating untrammelled egoism. Blackstone, for example, writing about self-defence, said that the 'public peace' was a 'superior consideration to any one man's private property'. Moreover, if private force were permitted as a remedy for private injuries, 'all social justice must cease', because the strong would rule over the weak.[5] Locke's use of the term 'property' has given rise to the suspicion that he favoured 'property above people', but he uses the term to refer to the lives and liberties of individuals. In the language of the time, slaves were said to lack property in themselves. Far from celebrating egoism, Locke thought that 'Self-love will make men partial to themselves and their Friends'. Moreover, 'ill Nature, Passion and Revenge will carry them too far in punishing others'. Government was necessary 'to restrain the partiality and violence of men'.[6] Adam Smith left no room for doubt about his own hopes:

> to feel much for others, and little for ourselves, that to restrain our selfish, and to indulge our benevolent, affections, constitutes the perfection of human nature; and can alone produce among mankind that harmony of sentiments and passions in which consists their whole grace and propriety.[7]

For Montesquieu too, liberty was not the mere satisfaction of desires. Political liberty 'in no way consists in doing what one wants'. In a society with laws, 'liberty can consist only in having the power to do what one should want to do'. Independence and liberty were different, said

Montesquieu. Liberty is the right to do everything not prohibited by law, not the right to do anything whatsoever.[8] Similarly, Locke famously insisted that liberty was not a 'state of licence'.[9] Plainly, for these writers moral norms outvoted subjective preferences.

Individual liberty: Liberals held that it was in the public interest for the government to create a sphere of individual initiative—a sphere of freedom from government or other collective supervision. There was to be freedom of speech, thought, the press, conscience, travel and association. The state would protect everyone from private force including monopolists. It was to everyone's advantage if all were able to co-operate freely and apply their talents as each thought best in the light of their own unique experience. The great Enlightenment philosopher Immanuel Kant explained it like this. He warned that human inclinations made it impossible for people to co-exist for long in a state of 'wild freedom'.[10] Despite the 'apparent wisdom of individual actions here and there', history revealed a good deal of 'folly and childish vanity' and often 'childish malice and destructiveness'.[11] And yet, the development of innate abilities could only be achieved in a society with the greatest personal freedom and 'therefore a continual antagonism among its members'. The circle could be squared only by 'the most precise specification and preservation of the limits of this freedom in order that it can co-exist with the freedom of others'.[12] To explain what he meant by antagonism he referred to the *'unsocial sociability* of men', the built-in human tendency to 'live as an individual' but also to 'live in society'.[13]

Science provides an example. Here we find individualism within an organised community is fully developed. Individual scientists may depart from the accepted view but must accept the discipline of proving to others that they are right. Challenges to the consensus are in theory, if not

9

always in practice, welcomed and scientists are expected to be disinterested in the final outcome, which will be the product of many minds working together in a spirit of friendly-hostile co-operation, in Sir Karl Popper's famous phrase.

As we have seen, the liberal commitment to individual freedom is the idea that critics have fastened onto, typically claiming that it is no more than a disguise for unfettered selfishness. Kant agreed that selfishness could be a destructive force, but believed that such 'wild freedom' could be contained by the 'civil freedom' protected by a liberal constitution.

Legitimate means

Liberals held that the government should have a monopoly of compulsion subject to checks and balances and should make decisions only after free and open public deliberation.

Monopoly on force subject to limits: There was a need for an agency to protect everyone, not only from foreign enemies, but also from criminals. But it was recognised that coercive power could be abused and the liberal approach was to keep the use of compulsory powers within constitutional limits. First, the state had a monopoly on the use of force to prevent private interests from using power to serve their own ends. Second, this monopoly was subject to checks and balances by dividing the lawmakers (Parliament) from those who had executive powers (such as the police) and from the judges. Third, force was only to be used when advance notice had been given in the form of general laws. Rule by decrees, imposed as the ruler wished, was preferably ruled out altogether or permitted only in genuine emergencies. Fourth, laws must apply equally to everyone to discourage lawmakers from acting to advance their own narrow interests or those of favourite allies.

Free and open public deliberation: Liberal constitutions were not only designed to prevent governments from overstepping the boundaries of legitimate power, they were also designed to ensure that public deliberation was thorough and drew upon the best knowledge available. It should therefore be open, with as little secrecy as possible, and anyone should be free to contribute. As Milton and Locke remarked, this commitment to public discussion implied a belief in the possibility of learning from each other through reasoned discussion.[14]

However, the early liberals were realistic about the possibilities of rational debate on religious questions. Some questions of faith, doctrine and even methods of church government had given rise to such heated and violent disputes that they were best kept outside the political realm. If public policy making was to be a process of seeking the best answers through discussion, criticism and openness to contradiction, religion was best confined to private life—the realm of conscience as Acton put it, not the realm of coercion. Only in this way could political life be a zone of compromise, give-and-take and mutual learning.

Liberals opposed the religious fanaticism that made claiming to speak for God useful to tyrants. Their solution was religious toleration, imperfectly begun by the Act of Toleration in 1689. It allowed protestant non-conformists their own places of worship and preachers so long as they took specified oaths of allegiance. But the method of encouraging toleration adopted in England seems to some observers to have been inconsistent. An established church headed by the monarch hardly seems neutral. However, the intention was to create a church that preserved beneficial Christian influence on public deliberation, including giving moral guidance to political leaders, but at the same time did not persecute rivals. The Church of England was given a privileged place from which to exert moral influence, but no political power to punish people of other faiths. It was an untidy compromise that has nonetheless worked quite well.

To summarise: first, the legitimacy of government should be based on the consent of the people being governed. Second, its ends should be to serve the common good and to protect individual liberty. And third, it should achieve its aims only by legitimate means. It should have a monopoly on the use of force subject to checks and balances. Compulsion should be exercised only through general laws applying equally to all, and not administrative decrees. Moreover, the constitution should encourage open discussion in order to add to the thoughtfulness of public policy making.

Assumptions about the human condition

One of the perennial tensions in political thought is between those who are optimistic and those who are pessimistic about the human condition and human potential. Are we, for example, 'fallen' and prone to sin to such a degree that the main human challenge is to put chains on our appetites? Or are we, despite imperfections, capable of scaling the heights of human accomplishment, if only political and social conditions give us the scope?

Liberals believed that humans were fallible but they differed from some thinkers, influenced by Plato in particular, who thought that the masses were fallible while the leaders—the philosopher kings—were not. Liberals were conscious of human limitations but believed we could create institutions to overcome our weaknesses. Experience of English monarchs had taught liberals that absolute power had a tendency to be abused, especially to favour special interests or royal favourites. Authoritarians and elitists, however, regarded the masses as fallible but not themselves. For liberals, rulers were not merely as fallible as everyone else, but especially vulnerable because power added to their temptations.[15]

But it was not only that self-interest encouraged the abuse of power, liberals also thought that ignorance, superstition and bigotry were more likely to flourish under a closed system. Hence they encouraged open government. Locke rebutted the epistemological basis for unlimited power by showing that no one was entitled to be so sure of his knowledge that it legitimised absolute rule over others. The liberal solution was that no one should be permitted absolute power on any ground, including professed moral or intellectual superiority. There should be oversight of rulers and open government. Milton had defended free discussion, based on the idea that public disagreement can be creative. Locke rebutted the false certainty offered by revealed knowledge or claims made in his own day that knowledge was innate. Even the most educated person had only a partial understanding, he said: 'We are all short sighted, and very often see but one side of a matter... From this defect I think no man is free. We see but in part, and we know but in part.'[16] Locke wrote about educating the young and emphasised the importance of encouraging a disinterested attitude to seeking truth. They should, he said, not be taught the arts of defending an entrenched view, but rather the skills needed to judge the true from the false.[17] As he argued in *Conduct of the Understanding*, to be 'indifferent which of two opinions is true, is the right temper of mind that preserves it from being imposed on, and disposes it to examine with that indifferency, until it has done its best to find the truth'. But, he said, 'to be indifferent whether we embrace falsehood or truth or no, is the great road to error'.[18]

The fear that a closed system of government would lead to bigotry was intimately associated with experience of religious fanaticism. The liberal solution was not only the religious toleration described earlier, based on keeping religion in private life and denying fanatics the power to coerce others, but also the encouragement of religious toleration within the 'realm of conscience' itself. Religions should teach toleration and be prepared to live in peace with other faiths, so long as they genuinely share the same tolerant approach.[19] They could believe firmly in their own doctrines, criticise other faiths and try to win converts but without abandoning their own spirit of self criticism.

Because of their expectations about the benefits that would flow from an open and competitive society, liberals attached great weight to education. But it had to be education of the right kind, designed to encourage objectivity, self-criticism and basic respect for the holders of other opinions.

To summarise: liberals were wary of excessive concentrations of power, public or private, because they feared human fallibility. Consequently, in the provision of goods and services there should be competition to discourage monopoly; democracy was preferred over authoritarianism so that rulers could be replaced; the state with its monopoly of force should be subject to constitutional limits; and decisions should be made after open, public discussion. Similarly the absolute certainties of religion were restrained by exposure to doubt, criticism and the systematic, shared learning of science.

What kind of society did they expect to emerge under liberalism?

Liberals thought that in a free society human knowledge and civilisation would advance and that poverty and hardship

14

would be much reduced. In the eighteenth and nineteenth centuries liberals in Parliament tended to oppose the 'unearned' inequality of people with inherited landed estates, but were not against inequalities that had been earned. They did not object to success if it had been acquired through honest endeavour, which meant that it was likely to be the result of success in providing for others, a good thing in itself. But more important still, liberals of Adam Smith's generation favoured the creation of wealth through enterprise because they believed it would benefit everyone, including the lowest ranks of the people.[20] Liberals believed that what lay ahead in a free society was an era of boundless discovery in science, agriculture, medicine and manufacturing.

The true nature of the political process

Liberals have typically argued that there is something about government or the political process as such that makes failure inevitable, or at least more likely. John Stuart Mill put it like this:

> in all the more advanced communities the great majority of things are worse done by the intervention of government, than the individuals most interested in the matter would do them ... if left to themselves. ... all the means which it possesses of remunerating, and therefore of commanding, the best available talent in the market—are not an equivalent for the one great disadvantage of an inferior interest in the result.[21]

Are his claims still justified? The essential characteristic of the state is that it exerts legitimate compulsion. The alternative is not, therefore, merely the voluntary exchange of goods at agreed prices (a market), but voluntary co-operation of all forms, whether inspired by religious faith, philanthropy, family loyalty, self-interest or mutual benefit. To speak of the market as the alternative often awakens animosity, largely because the market is associated with a self-regarding interest in making money. Moreover, in recent years the champions of the market have harmed its reputation by willingly accepting that it rests primarily on self-regard. As John Kay has convincingly argued in *The Truth About Markets*, the market process is valuable by comparison with political authority, not because of self-interest (which in any event is found in abundance in political systems) but because it is a system of voluntary co-operation and pluralism rather than compulsory co-ordination. To avoid confusion and to make clear the vital characteristic of the alternative, I will refer to pluralistic or unforced systems rather than market systems because they are only one form the unforced alternative might take. The tendency to treat the market—the system of mutual bargains based on money—as the alternative to state welfare has contributed to a common confusion, namely that the state represents altruism. But it represents no such thing. The government has no money of its own, only that of other people and its primary method of operating is not voluntary.

The defining characteristic of the state—democratic politics in our country—therefore, is legitimate compulsion. That is, individuals are elected or appointed and have the political authority to make decisions, subject to rules. There are winners and losers, and the winners can enforce their decisions on everyone. All members of society must pay for hospitals and schools provided by the government, whether they approve of its policies or not. We accept this degree of coercion because the authority to coerce can change hands. The hope of being able to coerce others in our turn leads us to accept coercion by them for the time being.

It is true that some things have to be decided and enforced by the state. Laws defining acceptable behaviour should apply equally to all and some services may also be best provided by the government. Policing, for example, is properly a public service. But in health and education the government has extended the authority of the state beyond its capabilities.

In a system of voluntary co-operation—an unforced system—the power to decide lies in the hands of people who are, in effect, conducting small-scale experiments in how best to set up and make a success of schools, hospitals or other services. They cannot force their decisions on anyone else. Private schools, for example, decide what the school will teach, who they will admit, and the fees to be charged, and then offer themselves to parents who have the final say about where to send their child. There is no coercion—no winner takes all. The key to success is having something that parents want. The schools may be willing to teach only in a certain way (especially when run by a church) and, if they cannot attract pupils, some would rather close down than abandon their standards, but they can not compel anyone to accept their approach. Similarly, parents can't coerce schools or other parents. They each make their own decisions. A good deal of mutual adjustment follows, perhaps reluctantly in some cases, but there is no imposition of one solution on all.

The problems that make the government unsuitable for running services like health and education fall into three groups. The first two are connected with the nature of modern politics and the third is a consequence of monopoly, a disadvantage not unique to the government sector.

First, modern democracy involves a struggle for power. Democratic politics tends to turn into a fight between factions that try to build up loyalties, often resembling tribalism. This kind of entrenched struggle for power tends to produce a tightening of central control at the expense of local discretion so that the ruling party can impose its views and demonstrate to voters that it has been effective, either by informing them of real accomplishments or deceiving them. In practice those who win power are inclined to treat their election victory as a temporary licence to exercise the powers of a dictator.

The need to stand for election is supposed to make the government responsive to the people, but the desire to win the next election also has an impact on the way power is used. The ruling party will need to show that it had clear aims and that they have been achieved. As under the Blair/Brown regime, this means that it must set central goals for areas such as health and education and establish systems to ensure that they are implemented by those with the day-to-day power in the schools and hospitals. However, in all large organisations, whether public or private, the senior managers have to deal with the reality that employees who carry out the work of the organisation have knowledge and skills not easily possessed by the chief executive, and may well have different motives or objectives. As a result, the chief executive who wants to impose central aims tends to establish rules and systems for monitoring and reporting to the centre to ensure compliance. These rules restrict the discretion of doctors and teachers, without necessarily improving standards in any real sense.

For example, the Government required Accident and Emergency departments to discharge patients within four hours of arrival. In some cases patients were kept waiting outside A&E in ambulances because the four-hour period did not start until patients entered A&E.[22] The Key Stage tests for school children are now acknowledged to have had a similar perverse effect and the Government plans to replace them. Increased performance may have been the result of 'teaching to the test' rather than real improvements in attainment. Good teaching depends on the skill of the teacher in face-to-face situations with children. Remote central controls or enforced compliance with targets can prevent effective teaching.

The second characteristic of modern British politics is that political decisions often involve compromises between contending groups, some of whose aims are mutually incompatible. Typically they are compromises between rival groups with influence on the ruling party, perhaps internal factions, or outside organisations such as trade unions, businesses or pressure groups. Decisions are sometimes made and imposed on schools or hospitals to appease a pressure group when they may not be compatible with other government objectives. In some cases, measures encounter opposition but are introduced in a weakened form that achieves little. Foundation hospitals, for example, were established despite opposition to their very existence, but their powers of independent action were severely limited. So it was with the trust schools created by the Education and Inspections Act of 2006. When there are mutually incompatible objectives, we often learn more by letting the protagonists try out their ideas in competition with each other. All can then learn from the successes and failures that follow, whereas imposed compromises tend to suppress such mutual learning.

Two features of the unforced alternative stand out: pluralism and critical enquiry. By pluralism I mean a system that allows many people to follow their own judgements and offer members of the public better ways of doing things, which they can accept or reject. I have emphasised critical enquiry as a separate characteristic to stress the importance of open debate in learning from both successes and failures. Experimentation on its own—mere diversity for its own sake—would not necessarily lead to widespread improvement unless accompanied by a spirit of free enquiry, public debate, openness to contradiction and a willingness to abandon failed experiments in favour of more promising rivals.

It is common to complain that markets—just one element in an unforced system—only benefit the rich, and it is indeed always an advantage to have money in your pocket. But politics too has some built-in biases against the poor. In particular, it pays to be well organised rather than disorganised. Campaigns need to be funded and supporters kept happy. It is, therefore, an advantage in politics as well as in markets to have money. Moreover, insiders (the ruling party and officials) have a strong advantage over outsiders (voters and opposition parties) because the insiders control the information that allows their own efforts to be evaluated. It is no exaggeration to claim that the solitary man or woman with little understanding of public affairs and with little money in the bank, is more likely to find a good school or hospital in an unforced system than under a state monopoly. But it is not merely getting the government out of the way that counts. Rather, the government should be restricted to what it can do best in the provision of schools and hospitals, namely guaranteeing access for all without public-sector monopoly.

The third group of problems result from the use of concentrated and exclusive power. As Mill has argued, the over-concentration of power tends to have five main (sometimes overlapping) consequences:

1. experimentation with alternatives is suppressed, which means that improvements are less likely to occur, the rate of growth of new knowledge slows down and the ability to react to changes in external events is reduced.

2. there are fewer outside experts with the knowledge to criticise, hence official errors can more easily persist and power can more easily be abused.

3. opportunities in the wider population for personal development are reduced, further curtailing the potential for independent oversight.

4. ordinary citizens become more likely to look to the government to solve their problems instead of to their own idealism, energy and skill.

5. the ambitious people in society become more likely to seek employment in the government sector, thus accelerating still further the process whereby independent expertise is diminished.

Competition is the opposite of monopoly, but what is meant by competition? Sometimes the term is used by people who are making very different assumptions. Of all the academic disciplines, economics is the one most sympathetic to free enterprise, but there is more than one school of thought and one is heavily influenced by collectivist assumptions. Some economists understand competition by contrasting the real world of manufacturing, buying and selling with an ideal situation, that of 'perfect competition'. Essentially it is a state of affairs in which there are many suppliers, none of which is big enough to control the price; products are identical; and consumers and producers alike have full knowledge of prices and alternative products.

The rival view, associated especially with Hayek, is that competition should be understood, not by comparing the real world with an ideal situation, but as a voyage of discovery. The prices of goods and services remain to be discovered, not least because they are constantly changing. Our own preferences as consumers are changing as we learn more about what is on offer. It is not obvious in advance who will turn out to be good at making products or providing a service. Nor is it obvious in advance which products or services people will want. In this sense a competitive system resembles scientific discovery. It is a facet of an open, liberal society, which recognises that we learn how to improve human affairs by avoiding the over-concentration of power in a few hands and, instead, relying on free discussion and the clash of opinion as the best way of revealing the truth and finding better ways of overcoming problems and advancing civilisation.

Today the Government has begun to speak of competition (or contestability) in public services, and superficially it looks as if some of its members have become converts to market principles. But, in reality, they belong to the tradition that sees competition as a management technique to induce subordinates to behave as the chief executive requires. The NHS, for instance, has established a system of fixed prices to facilitate contestability, the NHS tariff, but in a fully competitive system it is precisely the prices that must be allowed to vary.

These objections to monopoly do not necessarily imply that the only alternative is private pluralism. A major explanation for government failure is that it has acted on a scale that has made evaluation of results and adaptation to failure or success more difficult. The great philosopher of the open society, Sir Karl Popper, wrote about the importance of developing a 'social technology' that would allow reforms to take place and to be improved and shaped as the results emerged. In particular, reforms should be on a scale small enough to allow cause and effect to be unravelled.[23] He was not opposed to government services and belonged in the tradition of social democracy. But he wanted reforms that genuinely improved conditions. He called his approach 'piecemeal social engineering' and contrasted it with 'utopian social engineering'. The command and control approach, by comparison, made it more difficult to establish whether a policy worked or not. There was a tendency to suppress criticism or to hide behind idealistic declarations. Critics were forced into silence by implying that they lacked idealism—they did not care enough. Such romanticism, warned Popper, has often led to drastic errors on a huge scale. Genuine concern for other people would be more likely to lead to reform on a human scale, thus permitting errors to be quickly spotted and corrected. Romantic exaggeration was often a disguise for autocrats who would tolerate no criticism.

The argument I am advancing is, therefore, not based on blanket animosity to government action. In the provision of services, however, monopoly is a danger to be avoided. Where a service should be provided by the government and where an element of local monopoly is unavoidable, then Popper's case for a social technology of reform becomes vital. Every effort should be made to facilitate comparisons, either by decentralisation to different localities or by encouraging the government sector to compare itself with alternatives.

A presumption against government interference?

Many can accept what has been said so far, but recoil a little from the assumption of non-interference made by many liberals. Surely, they say, government actions are often beneficial? Why advocate an automatic presumption against them?

Why did some writers in the liberal tradition speak of government interference as if they were always opposed to it? A few were utopians who hoped for a world without any force, but this was always a minority taste and does not explain why many leading writers have argued in favour of a presumption against 'interference'. Hayek's explanation is that they used this term only when referring to government as a 'service agency', not to its core role as protector of personal security. This distinction needs a little more explanation. Hayek follows Mill in distinguishing between the 'authoritative' and 'non-authoritative' roles of government: the first was concerned with controlling behaviour through threats of punishment; and the second with providing services for people financed from taxes.[24] Payment of taxes is compulsory, to be sure, but it is a lesser form of coercion, particularly if the service genuinely benefits those who pay the taxes.

Mainstream liberals have always accepted that the government can legitimately provide services for its people. In the *Wealth of Nations* Adam Smith argued that under a 'system of natural liberty' government had three main duties. The first two concerned personal protection. The government should protect citizens from invasion by foreign countries; and it should provide a system of justice to protect members of the society from criminals. The third duty acknowledged that the government could legitimately provide useful services. It could erect and maintain public works and institutions that would not be provided privately because the profit could never repay the expense, even though it might frequently 'do much more than repay it to a great society'.[25]

Smith had in mind two main types of public works. First, there were those necessary to promote the commerce of society, including roads, bridges and canals and the defence of trade in dangerous regions of the world. Such commerce would, he believed, increase wealth for everyone. Second, there were measures for promoting the 'instruction of the people', not only children but also people of all ages to ensure that they were able to play their part in the intellectual life of the society.

In the nineteenth century John Stuart Mill continued the debate about where to draw the line between the state and civil society. He gave three reasons for limiting 'non-authoritative' state services.

1. When private individuals could provide a better service, the state should not be involved.

2. Even if government officials could do a better job, there was still a presumption in favour of private provision as a means of educating people in the skills of voluntary co-operation. This reason, said Mill, was not so much a question of liberty but personal development.[26] He had in mind a wide range of activities, from industrial and philanthropic enterprise to jury trials and local government. Direct involvement in local organisations creates institutions and skilled people that serve as bulwarks against absolutism. A state 'that dwarfs its men, in order that they may be more docile instruments in its hands even for beneficial purposes', he said, 'will find that with small men no great thing can really be accomplished'.[27] He does not say that government has no useful role in the provision of services, but thinks it should act like a 'central depository' actively circulating the results of experiments. Its aim should be to 'enable each experimentalist to benefit by the experiments of others; instead of tolerating no experiments but its own'.[28]

3. There was a general presumption against adding too much to the government's powers, because the bigger it got, the greater its potential for harm. The more it does, the more it converts 'the active and ambitious part of the public into hangers-on of the government' or some party that hopes to become the government.[29] He gives the

example of Russia, which in his time was run by a highly centralised bureaucracy. The mass of people looked to it for direction and the ambitious for personal advancement. In such a society, where most people look to the state to solve their main problems, they 'naturally hold the state responsible for all evil which befalls them'.[30] Occasionally there may be a revolution and the supreme ruler may be changed, but the power of the bureaucracy remains, for few others have the knowledge or experience to run the key institutions. Ultimately such a concentration of talent is fatal to the bureaucracy itself, as it sinks into indolence in the absence of effective criticism by outsiders of equal ability and knowledge.

No absolute rule could be laid down to define the limits of government, Mill thought, but the benchmark against which to test all arrangements was this: 'the greatest dissemination of power consistent with efficiency; but the greatest possible centralisation of information, and diffusion of it from the centre'.[31] The government, that is, should be the servant of the independent sector not its rival.

How many people would seize the opportunity for greater personal development if it were offered? We can't be sure and, if Mill is correct, we must assume that the pervasiveness of the state will already have diminished the readiness of many people to take up additional challenges. On the other hand, there are still huge amounts of voluntary activity, and regular displays of enormous generosity to good causes. It may take time for the social fabric to be fully repaired but there are strong foundations on which to build.

Positive government!

The question that concerned liberals who followed Mill at the end of the nineteenth century was whether the state could assume a more positive role without endangering liberty. A group led by the Oxford philosopher, T.H. Green, advocated freedom in a more 'positive' sense, not merely the removal of hindrances to individual liberty. Freedom 'in the positive sense', said Green, was 'the liberation of the powers of all men equally for contributions to a common good'.[32]

By the 1870s the role of the state was already being extended and the doctrine of laissez faire seemed to many to be inadequate. In 1879, T.H. Green responded by putting forward a new rationale for liberalism that tried to place it on a morally more defensible footing than was offered by utilitarianism, the intellectual driving force behind laissez faire. Utilitarianism is the doctrine that believed the guiding principle of human conduct should be the greatest happiness of the greatest number, in Jeremy Bentham's famous phrase. There is no logical connection with laissez faire, but in practice its adherents in the early nineteenth century focused on sweeping away laws that they felt had been enacted for the benefit of a few wealthy people at the expense of the majority.

Utilitarianism treated human happiness as a primary purpose and Green accepted that during the first half of the nineteenth century it had been a reforming and progressive doctrine. By the second half, however, many people found it to be a defence of privilege. Green and his followers such as Ritchie and Bosanquet felt that the defence of liberty offered by utilitarianism was based on too shallow a view of human nature, especially because it offered too restricted a view about the purpose of government. The state might have been too intrusive when Bentham was writing but by the second half of the nineteenth century Green felt that its main purpose should be to create the conditions for individuals to lead a moral life. It should not try to create the good life for them but instead create conditions in which they could develop their benign capacities to the full and advance civilisation through their own free endeavours. It must not replace their efforts. He shared the concern of the utilitarians that the state might overstep its boundaries. It should not try to bring about human happiness and it should not try to make people morally good, but it should try to create the conditions in which the heights of benevolence could be attained.

Green made no concessions to socialist criticisms already being advanced, and defended private property, freedom of trade and freedom of bequests against those who attacked them. The increased wealth of one person, he said, was not necessarily at the expense of anyone else.[33] He accepted that the accumulation of capital had led to many people working as hired labourers, but there was nothing to prevent them from being educated or otherwise improving their lives, as many had done.[34] He accepted that there was a small impoverished and reckless proletariat, but not because of the system of wage labour as such. It was a legacy of serfdom and deferential rural labour.[35] The remedy was not to suppress economic freedom but to encourage education.

The test to be applied to any proposed government action or change in the law was pragmatic. Did it liberate individuals by increasing self-reliance or enhancing their ability to add to human progress? Naturally, Green's examples were drawn from his own day. If the object of government were for all people to be able to make the most of themselves, then he thought it legitimate to 'interfere' with working conditions fatal to health by limiting hours of work for women and children. He favoured public health measures to eliminate disease and he supported compulsory education. Would these aims not have been better attained by voluntary action? Green agreed that a society that protected health and secured education spontaneously was preferable but felt that we must take people as they are.[36] A law requiring a man to educate his child if he would have done so anyway will not be seen as a restraint but a 'powerful friend'.

The control of alcohol was an issue in the 1870s. Was control a short-cut that would be self-defeating? Would it not be better to wait until people came to accept voluntary self-restraint? Green thought it would be better to wait if waiting were a remedy, but believed that drunkenness was getting worse. In fact alcohol consumption was falling in the last quarter of the 19th century but Green argued that self-reliance and independence were not weakened by legal control but enhanced by it.

In the hands of later liberals Green's line of thought was considerably extended and it became difficult to distinguish liberalism from socialism, but at least until Hobhouse was writing (his *Liberalism* was published in 1911) there was a recognisable difference between a liberalism that Locke would have acknowledged and the emerging socialist theories that put no effective limit on what the state should do. Hobhouse distinguished between three types of socialism: official, mechanical and liberal.

By 'mechanical socialism' he meant Marxist theories that explained everything as the 'mechanical' outcome of economic relations. He used the term 'official socialism' to describe the Fabians and other centralisers who saw themselves as a superior class with a duty to win power and, for the good of the masses, impose their views through officialdom. Liberal socialism ought to be democratic, that is, it should come from below, not from a few superiors who believed they were above the rest. And second it must give the average citizen 'free play in the personal life for which he really cares'. It must make for the development of all the potential powers of an individual personality, not their atrophy or suppression.[37]

So, for Hobhouse and others like him, the state could be a liberator, helping to release individual talent and energy to improve social conditions for all. The state could be a force for good, allowing everyone to be the best that they could become. Unfortunately, this well intentioned idealism, despite being clearly distinguished from elitist and author-itarian brands of socialism by Hobhouse and T.H. Green, led many people to lower their guard over the next few decades. The great majority of young intellectuals between the wars and immediately after the Second World War were drawn to such ideals and, in the hope of creating a better life for everyone, unwittingly did surrender their power of autonomous action—more often the autonomy of others—to the centralised state.[38]

Today the challenge is to take forward the ideals of T.H. Green and Hobhouse without walking into the same trap. A somewhat neglected writer, Michael Polanyi, has suggested a distinction that helps to avoid doing so.

Private action for the public good

A defence of the tradition of liberty must be more than a scheme for reducing the scope of government. It must also provide a strategy for private action to supersede failed collectivism. Collectivists in the West try to give the impression that freedom from state supervision and state-provided services means nothing but the ability to pursue private hedonistic and self-regarding satisfactions. (In spite of the fact that private and self-regarding hedonism has emerged as the monstrous bedfellow of state supervision and public sector monopolies.) This caricature has become so pervasive that we need new words to combat it and Michael Polanyi has suggested 'public liberty' as distinct from 'private liberty'.[39] Private liberty referred to private pleasures, whereas public liberty is the name Polanyi used for unforced, non-government, non-political actions in pursuit of public purposes—the common good.

One of the mistakes that took root during the twentieth century was the association of public purposes exclusively with the state. But if the ideal of liberty deserves our admiration and commitment, it must involve more than a desire to satisfy our purely personal wants. It is noteworthy that totalitarian regimes, whether communist or fascist, reserve special hatred for public liberty. Communist Russia, for example, was tolerant of people who used their private time to get drunk, and the state turned a blind eye to a high level of drunkenness. But if journalists formed an association to encourage the media to print the truth, or university professors campaigned for the ability to pursue their studies without fear or favour, or if doctors formed a professional association to uphold ethical standards in medicine, the authorities cracked down. Such was their determination to maintain total control, no private activity for the common good was tolerated. In a genuinely free society, it is precisely this sphere of public liberty that should be nourished and strengthened.

The pioneers of freedom, from Locke to Mill, understood this need perfectly well and had far more in mind than defending mere private preferences or the simple making of money by providing goods and services. It is no coincidence that the high point of liberty in Britain—from the late eighteenth century until the early twentieth century—was also the high point of philanthropy and mutual aid. Classical liberals wanted to set creative talent and idealism free from dogmatism and control by others to allow anyone with the ability and inclination to find better ways of improving human life, whether in medicine, engineering, agriculture or industry. The need for better health care led to charitable hospitals and a network of primary care organised by

31

friendly societies.[40] The need for education led to the spread of schools to reach the vast majority of the population long before governments got involved. The need to provide for the poor over and above the minimum offered by the poor law, led to the flowering of charities, and the desire for independence in the face of misfortune led to mutual aid associations.

These organisations emerged because many people at the time believed their lives had a higher purpose. The point of life was not to pass the time with as little inconvenience and as much personal pleasure as possible. It was to do your bit to enhance the society to which you belonged, perhaps modestly by improving conditions in your own town or village, or if you were fortunate enough to have a special talent, to add to the advance of human civilisation in your chosen sphere. Some aspired to push out the frontiers of scientific knowledge, to vanquish disease, to build better bridges, or extend the best education to all. Others focused on discovering better ways of manufacturing goods or growing crops and still others on ending poverty in less fortunate countries. Many felt they had a vocation. Certainly they would have been taught by church or community leaders that if you had a talent it came with a solemn duty not to waste it. Some believed they had a calling to relieve poverty or spread the gospel, or perhaps a vocation linked to paid work, or maybe a modest duty to do their best for their family and immediate circle. The sense of higher purpose varied in its grandeur, but during the heyday of liberty it was a real force. Whether it was defined in religious terms, or in more secular language, there was a strong expectation that the ideal to aim for was to be of service to some objective or hope beyond immediate personal satisfactions. Historically liberty was the ideal of those who wanted to free human talent and energy for higher purposes in every walk of life. It continued to be the inspiration of later liberals like T.H. Green and Hobhouse, but today this tradition stands in urgent need of renewal.

Much debate has long assumed only two categories— commercial activity and political activity. As we have seen, most classical liberals recognised that there may be a legitimate role for the political sector in providing services for members of the public and, of course, commercial provision also has a part to play, but we should not neglect the role of the 'second public sector', made up of independent organisations that are neither political nor commercial, but motivated by philanthropy or mutual aid and guided by the noble purpose of serving others.

Society as a membership association

What principles should guide reform? The approach to be described is grounded in the liberalism that has emerged step by step since the seventeenth century, a view that assigns to the government some vital but limited tasks. In particular, government is assigned a monopoly on the use of force so that it can protect personal security. Because this monopoly creates the danger that the government itself will become a threat, it too is subject to limits set by parliament. Above all, it should proceed through well-understood laws applied equally to all. This variety of liberalism implies a free people living in the same land, all prepared to accept restraints for the common good of each. In the seventeenth century there was a sense that the whole people, acting through parliament, had framed a new system of government for itself. The Bill of Rights of 1689, which embodied some key elements of early liberalism, is written in the name of 'the lords spiritual and temporal and commons assembled at Westminster lawfully, fully and freely representing all the estates of the people of this realm'.

Despite the narrow franchise, there was a strong sense of common purpose and shared beliefs.

Locke used the word 'commonwealth' to describe such an independent community of people.[41] He described the essence of the English heritage of law and how it differed from the more authoritarian Continental tradition. We should have a 'standing rule to live by, common to every one of that society'. As a result, all were free to follow their 'own will in all things, where the rule prescribes not; and not to be subject to the inconstant, uncertain, unknown, arbitrary will of another'.[42] English law, in other words, was a method of protecting our right to use our time and energy as we thought best. The law provided a clear warning when force could be used and in all other respects left us free.

The strongest influence was a reaction against the years of religious conflict between Protestant denominations and Catholics. Instead of religious groups trying to win power to impose their views, liberals argued that it was best to leave religious disputes outside politics. The state should have a monopoly on the use of compulsion, but it should tolerate religious differences so long as they did not lead to violence or disorder. This was accomplished largely by legal silence on many matters of religious doctrine. The feeling was that some issues are best left outside the law, because no amount of discussion can resolve them. Hence liberals have called for a 'live and let live' society.

The English heritage of liberty is based on the idea of an independent community of people conceived as a kind of membership association that had founded a system of self-government to protect personal security, encourage open and democratic government, and provide for individual liberty under the law. Open and representative government is accomplished, not through majoritarian democracy, which implied enforcing fixed opinions, but by encouraging deliberative democracy—listening and reflecting before deciding. Individual liberty meant to be free to do anything not expressly prohibited by law, including the enjoyment of freedom of conscience and speech, the right to leave the country, and to move freely within it.

The system of liberal democracy evolved gradually based on these guiding principles. Periods of deep mistrust of the state produced laissez faire in the nineteenth century and romanticised over-confidence in government produced collectivism in the twentieth. Today the challenge remains.

The revival of interest in national loyalty today partly reflects awareness among those who align themselves with the left that the role of the state remains an unresolved question of our time. It is rather surprising that Gordon Brown and writers such as David Goodhart chose to use the term nationalism rather than patriotism.[43] The former term has often (rightly or wrongly) been associated with national aggression towards foreigners. Patriotism, however, has typically meant a legitimate love of country because its values—freedom, democracy, pluralism, religious tolerance —were worthy of it; or it has described a sense of allegiance to a country merely because we live there in the knowledge, not only that we depend on it but also that it relies on us. Nevertheless, the revival should be welcomed, not only because we find ourselves threatened by Islamist fundamentalists who hate the free and democratic systems of the West, but also because the nation has a legitimate role in providing, not just for the personal safety of every citizen, but also a welfare guarantee.

What should be the guiding principles for social security, education and health care? The underlying problem is that we have only partially progressed out of the age of collectivism, a period of narrow certainties that included the automatic association of 'caring' with the state and 'not caring' with the market. The origins of this notion lie in the association of freedom with selfish individualism.

To claim that a free society sets loose nothing but selfishness is in flat contradiction of the facts; and its corollary, that to politicise a walk of life removes selfishness, is plainly wrong. Selfishness is possible in all situations, public or private. Selfishness is a problem built in to the human condition: to combat it, the political sphere needs checks and balances, and civil society needs competition, pluralism and a spirit of critical inquiry.

Three legitimate roles for government

During the twentieth century Hayek developed Mill's thinking. He tried to identify the character of government activity that was incompatible with freedom. Governments may prohibit harmful actions by law and, like Adam Smith, he thought they could provide services in order to widen the possible methods of co-operation available. The doctrine of a 'government of laws', Hayek argued, was intended to deny governments the method of issuing specific orders or prohibitions directed at known individuals, as if it were an army commander.[44]

Writing at about the same time as Hayek, H.L.A. Hart distinguished between, on the one hand, laws that prohibited or required specified conduct on pain of punishment and, on the other, laws that facilitated human action, including laws relating to companies, contracts, wills and marriages.[45] Like Hayek, he pointed out that this second type of law created institutions that could be used by people to improve their own lives. Law in the first sense was about exerting control but in the second, it was about creating useful frameworks for free enterprise.

Drawing on these writers, and if we accept that the government is characterised by its use of legitimate coercion, we can now say that there are three main uses of its coercive powers: enacting and enforcing laws to guide conduct, creating legal facilities to aid social co-operation, and raising taxes to provide services. Each has different implications.

The first involves the most fundamental use of coercion: laws applying equally to all that prohibit or require a type of behaviour on pain of punishment.

The second type of law is not coercive to the same extent. Governments also create legal institutions or 'facilities' that can be used by free citizens to run their affairs. The best examples of the law as a facilitator of freedom are company law, charity law and the law of marriage and inheritance. The whole system of civil law can also be looked upon in a similar light. In this case the state essentially provides a framework for the settling of private disputes.

Third, the government can require compulsory payment for public services. In this 'service' capacity a number of variations are possible. For present purposes five can be distinguished:

1. *Everyone pays taxes because everyone may benefit:* For example, the government imposes an obligation to meet the cost of the state safety net. We have had a national minimum for many years. Because it is available to all, it is reasonable to expect everyone to contribute even though the need will never arise for many.

2. *Everyone pays taxes because everyone does benefit:* The state may impose an obligation to pay for a service provided by the government itself because all benefit from it. Policing is one such example.

3. *The user pays because only the user benefits:* For example, user charges are required by the government but not imposed on all taxpayers, only on service users, such as road tolls imposed on drivers.

37

4. *Compulsory insurance to avoid <u>imposition</u> on other people:* The government imposes an obligation to spend on a specific thing to prevent private individuals from imposing costs on other people, often called 'free riding'. Third-party car insurance is the most obvious example. In some other countries health insurance is also obligatory.

5. *Everyone pays but the government gives back <u>limited spending authority</u>:* The government may impose an obligation to pay taxes, and then return the money in the form of a limited authority to buy a service, subject to conditions. Education or nursery vouchers are prominent examples. The justification for this approach is that some people cannot afford services considered vital, such as the education of children, and so the state ensures that everyone has a guaranteed amount of spending power while avoiding public sector monopoly.

3

Independence and Welfare

The Department for Work and Pensions' current Five Year Strategy identified two problems.[1] First, there was a pool of persistently economically inactive people of working age, especially lone parents and those on Incapacity Benefit (IB). And second, there was too much child poverty. The Government has repeatedly affirmed its view that the best way out of poverty is work and has declared its intention of increasing the number of lone parents in work by 300,000 and the number of IB recipients in work by one million. John Hutton, Secretary of State for Work and Pensions until 2007, even declared war on the 'can work, won't work culture'.

The Government's green paper, *In Work, Better Off*, published in July 2007 acknowledged the 'stubborn barriers' to the goal of full employment. Over three million people of working age had been on benefits for over a year, many on Incapacity Benefit. And there were three million households, involving 1.7m children, in which no one was working. The guiding principles of reform were 'rights and responsibilities', which meant among other things that people on benefits should 'help themselves get into work'; there would be more personalised help and advice; and there would be partnership with the voluntary and private sectors.

The overall aim was to increase the employment rate from 75 per cent of people of working age to 80 per cent. Another 300,000 lone parents should be brought into the workforce via a 'new social contract' and up to one million recipients of Incapacity Benefit should be able to find work, especially via Pathways to Work, a programme offering practical help and advice.

The Government appears to believe that work-focused interviews for lone parents can achieve little more and since October 2008 those whose youngest child is 12 or over can no longer claim Income Support solely because they are lone parents. They are expected to work or transfer to Job Seekers Allowance, where pressure to work will be stronger. From 2010 lone parents whose youngest child is seven or older will no longer be able to claim Income Support.

All recipients of benefit who are capable of work will have to frame a back-to-work action plan after three months and if they are still out of work after 12 months they will be referred to a specialist private contractor, whose task will be to help and support them into a job. If that fails they will be required to undertake full-time work experience.

In a speech to the Social Market Foundation in February 2008, Work and Pensions Secretary James Purnell, reaffirmed his commitment to the plan and announced that everyone classified as long-term unemployed would be expected to take active steps to find work including 'work related activity in return for their dole'.

What's Wrong With Current Policies?

The weaknesses in current policies have been understood for a long time. Harvard's Professor David Ellwood (who was to become an adviser to President Clinton) when writing in the mid-1980s concluded that welfare caused conflict because it treated symptoms not causes. There were two undesirable effects. First, when you give people money, you reduce the pressure on them to work and care for themselves. No one, he said, 'seriously disputes this proposition'. Second, the low income of single-parent families has been tackled by providing welfare support, 'yet such aid creates a potential incentive for the formation and perpetuation of single-parent families'. Current policies in Britain are producing both these effects.

Self-sufficiency is discouraged

Since 1997 the Government has consistently questioned the doctrine of one-sided welfare rights and argued that we had both rights and responsibilities: if you can work you should. But, if you add together the people on welfare benefits and working tax credit, there were more in 2008 than in 1997.[2]

In November 1997 there were 5.4m people of working age on benefits plus 731,000 recipients of family credit, a total of 6.1m. In February 2008 there were 5.2m people of working age on benefits and in April 2008, 2.1m on working tax credit, a total of 7.3m.[3] The key distinction is not between a welfare benefit and a tax credit but between income that has been earned by working and income that has been taken from all taxpayers and transferred to particular individuals.

The Institute for Fiscal Studies (IFS) has compared the amount received from net state benefits with the amount paid in personal taxes. In 2008-09 45 per cent of families in the UK received more in cash benefits and tax credits (all cash benefits, tax credits, SERPS and S2P) than they paid in personal taxes (income tax, national insurance and council tax). In 1979 it was 35 per cent.

Many people on tax credits are also receiving more in benefits and credits than they earn from work, allowing for any income tax and national insurance (NI) they pay. In 2008/09 a lone parent with two children under 11, not paying for childcare and earning £100 a week, would take home £317.52 of which £217.52 was benefits and tax credits. A lone parent with two children under 11, paying childcare of £50 a week and earning £175 a week, would receive £372.73 of which £217.22 was benefits and tax credits, allowing for income tax and NI.[4]

The IFS has calculated that in 2008/09 27 per cent of families in the UK (about 11 million adults) received more in net state benefits than from private income.[5] Many such families were pensioners but 1.089 million were lone parents. In 2008/09 58 per cent of lone parents received more in net state benefits than from private earnings. Couples with children were more likely to be self-sufficient: only 11 per cent of such families received more in net state benefits.

The figures have fluctuated over time. In 1979 49 per cent of lone parents received more in net state benefits than from private income. By 1988 the figure was 64 per cent and by 1996/97 71 per cent. The fall to 58 per cent is partly because more lone parents have taken a job and partly because of the steady economic growth over that period.

Overall, the impact of tax credits is mixed. For lone parents it encourages them to take a job rather than to remain on income support, but it discourages full-time work and penalises living as a couple, which would make self-sufficiency more likely.

It is sometimes said that tax credits are justified because they at least require some work rather than none. This argument is true, but tax credits also discourage recipients from increasing their hours of work and improving their earnings per hour by acquiring skills or taking on workplace responsibilities. It has long been known that tax credits reduce the incentives for improving skills and earnings. Alex Bryson and colleagues found that lone mothers on family credit were likely to be earning less than others not on family credit but with similar educational qualifications. They compared a sample of lone parents on family credit with those in work but not claiming in two years: 1991 and 1995. By 1995, the family credit recipients were earning 37 per cent less per week than non-recipients, allowing for 'their human capital and other characteristics'.[6] This disparity was partly due to the number of hours worked, but a significant difference of 28 per cent remained for hourly earnings. The authors concluded that family credit may discourage lone mothers from improving their skills or seeking promotion. As Jane Millar and her colleagues concluded from the same evidence, family credit gives a 'significant boost to income in work but this may be at the cost of preventing people from improving their long-term earnings capacity'.[7]

Marsh and McKay also concluded that family credit improved incentives to get a paid job in the first place but at the expense of reducing the incentives of those with jobs to work more hours or take a better-paid job. In their own words, 'while family credit clearly offers help with the first step—getting a job at all—it may act as a hindrance to further steps—improving earnings by overtime, promotion, or a second earner'.[8] According to Marsh, the consequence was that 'in-work benefits may re-create in work the poverty and dependence they are supposed to abolish out of work'.[9] Despite the availability of this evidence, when the Government came to power it extended the use of tax credits.

Couples are disadvantaged

Worse still, there is a couple penalty. If we take as a starting point a lone mother with a potential partner, according to the Institute For Fiscal Studies (IFS), if the lone mother earns £10,000 and the partner £25,000, they are £5,473 per year better off if they tell the authorities that they live separately. (22 per cent of the potential partner's income.) If the lone mother earns nothing and the potential partner earns £20,000 they are £4,522 better off if they live separately. (23 per cent of the potential partner's income.)[10]

Potential couples on low incomes (precisely those who can only make ends meet by combining their efforts) are discouraged from partnering (or re-partnering). As Mike Brewer of the IFS says, 'it is unfair to lone parents that they see such a considerable reduction in state support when they begin to cohabit'.[11]

How many people are affected? The IFS reported in March 2006 that the Government was paying tax credits or out-of-work benefits to about 200,000 more lone parents than the Office for National Statistics estimated to be living in the UK. The IFS concluded that it was highly likely that fraud explained much of the disparity.[12] Many lone parents re-partner despite the financial pressures. The Department for Work and Pension's destination of benefit leavers survey for 2004 found that 23 per cent left to re-partner.[13] For many, their decision to live together was a triumph of romance over economics. From their behaviour we can conjecture that, without powerful economic incentives to live separately, re-partnering would have been more common.

Discrimination is not only confined to working tax credit. The tax-benefit regime as whole also penalises couples. Using OECD data for 2006, Don Draper and Leonard Beighton have calculated that a one-earner married couple with children on the average full-time wage paid 40 per cent more tax in the UK than the OECD average.[14] They also compared the position of one-earner couples on the average wage with single people without dependents on the same earnings. In other OECD countries the tax paid by a one-earner married couple was 56 per cent of the tax paid by a single person without dependents. In the UK the figure was 75 per cent. In some countries the difference was striking. In the USA, for example, one-earner couples paid tax amounting only to 20.5 per cent of that paid by a single person: a single-earner couple with two children on the average wage paid tax worth 4.8 per cent of their income, whereas in the UK it was 20 per cent.[15]

To sum up: two problems remain. First, despite saying that work is the best way out of poverty, the Government's policies discourage full-time work by subsidising individuals who work as few as 16 hours a week. Second, the Government has failed to recognise that for people on low incomes with children, self-sufficiency is only possible by living as a couple.

Child poverty reduction—treating symptoms not causes

The Government's policy of reducing child poverty contradicts its aim of increasing the number of people in employment. Income has been transferred to households with children whether they work or not. Income support (paid only to claimants who are not working), for a lone parent with one child under 11 increased in real terms from 1997 to 2003 by over 19 per cent and for a couple with two children under 11 by over 31 per cent.[16] Any increase in income that can be obtained without working will tend to discourage people from taking a job.

Uncontrolled immigration has lowered wages for the poor

The Government has been encouraging large-scale immigration and ignoring its impact on the ability of people to fight their way to independence through work. This was something of a taboo topic for a long time, but fortunately in 2006 we were given permission to talk about it when Polly Toynbee dealt with low pay in an article in the *Guardian*.[17]

On any controversial topic it is common to find armies of academics arguing about the facts. Studies of the effect on wages of immigration are no exception and some researchers claim to find that immigration reduces wages and some that it does not. The most convincing studies show that the evidence has been that an increase in the supply of unskilled labour leads to a fall in wages for the low paid. For example, a study of the impact of migration into the USA between 1979 and 1995 by George Borjas of Harvard University concluded that immigration had reduced the wages of unskilled workers (those without American high-school diplomas) by five percentage points.[18]

A UK study for the Low Pay Commission looked at the impact of immigration between 1997 and 2005 and concluded that the arrival of economic migrants benefited workers in the middle and upper part of the wage distribution, but placed downward pressure on the wages of workers on lower levels of pay. Over the period, wages at all points of the wage distribution increased (presumably reflecting the growth rate in the economy as a whole) but Professor Dustmann and his colleagues from University College London (UCL) concluded that wages in the lowest quartile would have increased faster without the effect of immigration. They estimated that for each one per cent increase in the ratio of immigrants to natives in the working age population there was a 0.5 per cent decrease in the wages of the lowest tenth of workers.[19]

The historical trend

How does welfare dependency today compare with recent history? In 1951 just over three per cent of the population received national assistance or unemployment benefit. In 2006/07, not including the state pension, 23 per cent of households relied on income-related benefits.[20]

Nor is growing in-work dependency a matter of 'topping up' largely private incomes. In 2006/07, 29 per cent of households received half or more of their income from the state and 58 per cent of households with at least one adult over the pension age relied on the state for half or more of their income. Family breakdown is one of the main causes.

Only eight per cent of couples with two children receive half or more of their income from state benefits, compared with 63 per cent of lone parents with two children.[21]

The Government's estimates of the number of 'workless households' help to amplify the picture. Workless households are those of working-age with no one aged 16 or over in employment. In Spring 1997 there were 3.271m workless households (17.9 per cent of all households). In 2001 there were 3.060m (16.3 per cent) and in the quarter from April-June 2008 3,056m (15.8 per cent).[22]

The current strategy of the Government is to 'make work pay', but it is very unlikely to achieve its declared aim of reducing benefit dependency. In his February 2008 speech, James Purnell said he wanted people to be 'authors of their own lives'. Freedom from 'dependence of any sort' was the objective. Unfortunately the solutions offered so far do not match his hopes.

Welfare dependency has been worsening since the 1960s. In 1949/50 all social security benefits cost 4.7 per cent of GDP. A decade later the figure was still only 5.5 per cent, but by 1969/70 it had gone up to 7.1 per cent. Ten years further on it had reached 9.0 per cent and the post-war peak was in 1993/94 when it hit 12.6 per cent, reflecting the high unemployment following Britain's participation in and departure from the Exchange Rate Mechanism.[23]

After the introduction of working tax credit in 2003 it has become more difficult to track benefit expenditure because the Treasury treats payments of working tax credit as negative tax revenue. The most reliable estimate of expenditure on benefits is based on the cost of 'social protection'[24] in HM Treasury's Public Expenditure Statistical Analyses. In 2006/07 social protection expenditure was 13.4 per cent of GDP.[25] Both the main political parties must accept responsibility. Until recently they have been unwilling to impose obligations on benefit recipients and relied too heavily on 'making work pay' to the exclusion of other strategies.

The fatal flaw in all the discussions about removing barriers and making work pay is that they distract from the real problem that still remains to be resolved. The Government half acknowledges this reality when it speaks of rights and responsibilities, but it has so far failed to clarify what we can reasonably expect when help is made available. Until clear expectations are laid down, policy will continue to alternate between taking a step forward and a step back.

Two Approaches

I am going to contrast two approaches: one sees poverty as a misfortune to be relieved by the wider society and the other focuses on the mutual obligations implied by a society as a 'membership association'.

Relief of poverty

To be in poverty is not just to lack money. The cash shortfall is the result of other problems and it can only be dealt with effectively by discovering what those problems are and solving them. Giving people money gives them less reason to solve their problems for themselves. In those cases where the problem can *only* be solved by them, then their dependency increases. Not all problems can be solved by the individual concerned. This is obviously true of people who become too ill or disabled to work. But there are many problems that can't be solved without the enthusiastic effort of the individual concerned. An effective welfare system should distinguish more carefully between the two situations.

Poverty is closely related to work effort. If we look at *Households Below Average Income 2006/07*, it shows the risk of being in poverty on the Government's definition (60 per cent of the contemporary median).[26]

Incidence of Poverty and Willingness to Work

Type of family and work	Risk of poverty (%)
Lone parent not working	58
Lone parent working part-time	19
Lone parent working full-time	7
Couple—both not working	68
Couple—one or both working part-time	47
Couple—one FT and one not working	20
Couple—one FT and one PT	3
Couple—both working FT	2

The conclusion is blindingly obvious: the more people work the less likely they are to fall below the government's poverty line. The Government understands this reality as well as anyone, but it remains reluctant to implement the full measures necessary to require full-time work, or at least sufficient work to be self-supporting.

Membership

We have long felt that we owe each other something merely because we all live in the same land. However, if we think of society as a kind of membership association, as we should, we need to define what we can reasonably expect of each other. The fundamental aim of a liberal society is to create personal security in the sense of protection from arbitrary force. But should material security be seen in a similar light, as a basic benefit of membership?

For at least the last 400 years we have always had a state safety net. Material help is available to everyone, because we never know who might need it. Some recent discussions have started from the assumption that the safety net has been an historically unvarying level of bare subsistence, and that the concept of relative poverty is a discovery of recent times. It is therefore worth noting that this has scarcely ever been either the theory or the reality of the safety net. Even the demonised regulations of the nineteenth-century poor law were explicitly based on the contemporary standard of living of the poorest-paid labourer. The rule was that someone whose income was provided by the poor law authorities should not be as well off as anyone who was working for a living. How generous the safety level should be, how it should be related to the standard of living of other people, and whether it should be the same safety level for all, or related to the person's standard of living before the need for the safety net arose, are all important questions. But social policy is certainly not advanced by a purely propaganda contrast between the progressive England of today, as a place in which governments have linked social security benefits to the general standard of living of the country, with benighted older England, as a place where people in need of state assistance had their benefits calculated on the basis of bodily survival.

Once a safety net is guaranteed, however, it is legitimate to expect every citizen to make provision against misfortune when able to do so. What should these expectations be? We can reasonably expect to make provision for the normal expenses of living, and for periods when expenditure will be high—most notably when children arrive—or when income is lower, especially during retirement. If children are expected, any plan will need to include a permanent partner to allow for the children to be both cared for and supported financially by work (whatever division of labour there is between the two parents). Provision also needs to be made against misfortunes such as the early death of a partner, or illness, which may both reduce income and increase expenditure.

Theories assuming that people are largely victims of circumstance, or at the mercy of 'barriers', tend to speak of 'low pay' as if it were something entirely outside the influence of individuals. But the rate of pay depends in part on skills acquired and willingness to move jobs or to change locality in order to command a higher wage. And the number of hours worked can be increased either through overtime or a second job, or another household member taking a job. As shown above, the vast majority of people who escape poverty do so because they work hard and use their freedom to make the most of the conditions they find themselves in.

A certain amount of household expenditure is necessary for simple survival. B. Seebohm Rowntree distinguished between primary poverty, a state of affairs in which basic necessities could not be bought with the income available, and secondary poverty, which meant that the income was available for necessities, but was wasted on things he considered inessential. The straitened conditions in which some people live are often the result of unwise expenditure. According to deterministic theories, however, to say as much is to 'blame the victim'. Of course, the structure of the household may be outside individual control, for example, when a partner is widowed or deserted. It is also true that a number of people are born with few advantages and, however hard they try, they are unlikely to be able to earn a high income.

To summarise: with due allowance for factors beyond individual control, it is reasonable to expect individuals to take personal responsibility for improving their income, controlling their expenses, selecting an economically and socially viable family structure, and providing against both misfortunes and lifecycle events. *The New Consensus on Family and Welfare* was written in the late 1980s by a group of American academics including Michael Novak and Charles Murray. They argued that the probability of remaining in poverty is low for those who follow three rules: (1) attend school and gain some qualifications; (2) once an adult, get married and stay married and (3) stay employed, even at a wage and under conditions below your ultimate aims.[27]

The British welfare state was not built on their view. It was founded on paternalistic expectations of what people could achieve. Step by step, the state took responsibility for decisions that would have been better left to individuals. Provision against sickness, the cost of primary medical care, and unemployment (for some) ceased to be voluntary in 1911. From 1920 most people had unemployment 'insurance', which was not insurance in the strict sense. Unfunded national insurance pensions followed under the 1925 Act.

From 1948 large families were subsidised, when people who could only afford a couple of children would have been better served by limiting their family. Personal responsibility for housing expenditure was also diminished. Instead of expecting people to move to affordable accommodation, council rents were subsidised and later cash benefits were paid. In 1967 a national scheme of rate rebates was introduced followed by a national scheme of rent rebates and allowances in 1972. In 1983 rent rebates and allowances became housing benefit.

In the 1940s and 1950s it was taken for granted that most men would work, and that couples who planned to raise children would get married in order to be self-sufficient as a family unit. However, it became possible during the 1970s to have a child outside marriage and to have enough to live on. Planning ahead in the sense of marrying a partner suitable to be a good father or mother became less important. Saving personally for the future ceased to make sense to many. Savers would simply find themselves living on the results of their abstemiousness without state benefits, while their neighbours who had not saved would enjoy the same standard of living as them from the state. Thus, for a very long time public policy has been based on very low expectations of human resourcefulness.

The Elements of an Effective Government Strategy

1. End the taxation of interest on savings.[28]

2. End churning: let taxpayers keep more of their own money so that they can afford to pay for health care and education.

3. Restore provision against insurable contingencies, like ill health or certainties like death, to the independent sector.

4. Make welfare conditional by putting systems for supporting people out of work but capable of working on a more personal footing. At present, and despite recent policy shifts following the Freud report, they are primarily income maintenance systems. Instead they should become personalised services for the restoration of independence.

5. Scrap working tax credit and replace it with a hard-work top-up.

6. Replace income tax allowances with a system of income splitting that takes account of dependent children and

allows parents to share child care and work as they believe best.

7. Simplify state provision for old age so that the state's role is only to provide a national minimum.

8. Create family trust funds to help families provide for lifecycle events, such as having children and becoming older.

1. End the taxation of interest on savings

Some public policies narrow opportunities to escape from poverty. Taxation of interest on savings has an especially harmful effect on those who want to improve their conditions by saving from earnings. All taxation of income from savings should be abolished. If there is concern that wealthy people will benefit disproportionately, it would be feasible to introduce a separate tax threshold for income from savings—perhaps only the first £10,000 per year should be tax free.

2. End churning: let people keep more of their own money

According to the Office for National Statistics, policies of equalisation have led to the redistribution of income from a starting point of 15:1 to 4:1 when comparing the top 20 per cent of earners with the lowest 20 per cent. In 2006/07 households in the top quintile earned an average of £72,900. After adjustment for taxes and benefits they ended up with £52,400. Households in the bottom quintile earned on average £4,900, but after adjustment their final income was £14,400.[29] One of the more remarkable consequences of this massive equalisation is the extent to which many people in the middle of the income distribution and above pay personally for the cash and other benefits they receive from the government. How sensible is it for the government to take money from us and give it back as cash or services (after deducting its own costs)? Would it be more beneficial for people to make their own arrangements with their own money?

How much money flows back and forth from the same family in any one year? We can get some idea of the extent of this churning from figures regularly published by the Office for National Statistics. It divides the population up into tenths. Let's look at the sixth decile group (the group between the 50 per cent and 60 per cent marks based on unadjusted disposable income).

On average their original income (wages, salaries, interest and dividends) in 2006/07 was £25,104. Each household received from the government average cash benefits of £4,363, but also paid direct taxes (income tax, national insurance and council tax) of £5,620. Each household also paid on average indirect taxes (such as VAT and duties on alcohol, petrol and tobacco) of £4,742 and also received state services (benefits in kind such as the NHS and education) valued at £6,140.

In total, each household paid average taxes of £10,362 and received state benefits in cash or kind of £10,503. The average final income, after taking into account churning, was £25,245—£141 more than their market income.[30]

Looking at the average for a tenth of the population conceals some differences between households, but we can also repeat the exercise for family types. Let's look at a non-retired household made up of two adults and two children.[31] On average each earned £48,056. Direct taxes of £11,871 were paid plus indirect taxes of £6,806 (£18,677 in total). Benefits in kind (mainly health and education) were valued at £10,166 and each received state cash benefits of £3,086 (£13,252 in total). Taking everything into account, their average final income was £42,630, which means they paid £5,426 more in taxes than they received in benefits. Looked at another way, families with two adults and two children received benefits in cash and kind amounting to no less than 71 per cent of the average tax they had paid.

Taxes Paid and Benefits Received by Decile Group 2006/07

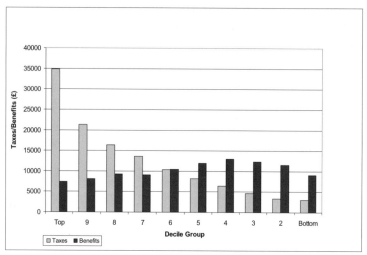

Source: Jones, F., 'The effects of taxes and benefits on household income, 2006/07', *Economic & Labour Market Review*, vol 2 no 7, July 2008, London: ONS.

Of course, we pay taxes for other useful public services, not least policing, the courts and defence. Nevertheless, many families are paying taxes at least equal to the cost of their own benefits. Such churning of money discourages independence. A more sensible general rule would be to aim for governments to leave cash in the hands of those who have earned it.

Based on disposable income unadjusted for household size we can see more clearly the extent of churning. The bottom decile paid taxes equivalent to 34 per cent of benefits received, the 2nd decile 29 per cent, the 3rd 38 per cent, the 4th 49 per cent and the 5th 69 per cent and the 6th 99 per cent. The top decile paid taxes worth over four times the value of benefits received but still benefited from benefits valued at £7,390. In Chapter 4 I will suggest how it might be possible to avoid churning for schooling.

3. Restore provision against insurable contingencies to civil society

The general principle proposed here is that if an event is insurable then cover is best provided by independent enterprise and not the state. If we apply Mill's criteria—if the service can be provided more effectively in civil society, or if it will provide opportunities for personal development and avoid adding unnecessarily to the size of government—then it should not be provided by the government. Mill, like Tocqueville before him, feared a society in which individuals looked too much to the state to solve problems, with the result that they became less capable of contributing to the continued advance of civilisation.

Three main contingencies can undermine efforts to be independent: loss of job, illness, and the premature death of the main breadwinner. Loss of income due to unemployment is not insurable, but loss of income due to illness or injury is and so too is the early death of the breadwinner. Of course, earning and caring for children may be divided between a man and a woman who live as a couple. Whether one of them is the 'main breadwinner' or not does not affect the argument—it is going to be a disadvantage if either one of them dies. Unemployment insurance has been provided for some groups, but the difficulty of distinguishing between voluntary and involuntary unemployment has prevented a purely private system from developing. For this reason support needs to be provided by government as part of its efforts to prevent hardship, to be discussed below.

Early death is covered by private life insurance and we know from past experience that private arrangements for insurance against loss of income during illness worked well. The aim of public policy should be to restore these services to civil society. The immediate candidates should be statutory sick pay and incapacity benefit.

In the past sick pay was provided by friendly societies far more satisfactorily than by governments now. The societies proved particularly effective at controlling fraud. Local control was the key to success.[32] Where local branches administered sick pay the members knew who was paying — it was the members themselves. But if a remote 'head office' made the payment, it was possible to entertain the illusion that no one was bearing the cost. For this reason, the friendly societies with local branches handled the problem of fraud far more effectively than modern welfare bureaucracies. Today many private insurers are already providing this service and could easily expand. Insurance would need to be obligatory — not to take personal responsibility from individuals but in keeping with Mill's strictures to prevent imposition on other people by individuals who failed to insure because they calculated that they would receive help anyway.

The main public policy problem will be how to cater for people who would like insurance but are not insurable because of pre-existing conditions. There are several possible solutions. For example, the government could forbid insurers from taking pre-existing conditions into account. Or a moratorium could apply, perhaps a stipulation that no claims can be made for twelve months during which time the state safety net would be available.

Under these proposals the government's role is transformed from one of taking responsibility for everyone to ensuring that no one is left out. It becomes a 'guarantor' rather than a service provider.

4. Make welfare conditional for people capable of work but not working

What principles should guide policy for people who are unemployed but capable of working? Should the government protect people from poverty or should the task be left to charity? And if there is a proper role for government, what should it be? A few libertarians say that government should not be involved at all and contend that all efforts to maintain a state safety net have been abused. The poor law was subject to a major reform in 1834 to overcome the harmful side-effects of the Speenhamland system of wage subsidisation. However, as the 1909 Royal Commission on the Poor Laws found, at the beginning of the twentieth century the number of people receiving poor relief was firmly under control at no more than four to five per cent of the population. Moreover, the poor law had not crowded out either private charity or mutual aid. In fact, they experienced their heyday when the poor law was in the background.[33]

Are there any lessons to be learnt from overseas? There have been a number of successful experiments in America, of which Wisconsin is the best known.[34] The main thrust was to insist on work. Education and training were not considered adequate substitutes. However, to ensure that an early return to work was a realistic possibility, Wisconsin found it necessary to create short-term subsidised jobs in the private and public sectors and to make available unpaid community work. Wisconsin Works or W-2 began in September 1997 as an implementation of the 1996 law that replaced Aid to Families with Dependent Children (AFDC) with Temporary Assistance for Needy Families (TANF). Six main principles can be identified:

1. Everyone who can work should work.

2. People not capable of total self-sufficiency should work within their abilities.

3. All policies should be judged by how well they strengthen the responsibility of both parents to care for their children.

4. The government should not reward behaviour it does not want more of, particularly out-of-wedlock births.

5. Benefits should not be an unconditional entitlement. They should reinforce behaviour that leads to independence.

6. Public policies should encourage communities, whether in the form of voluntary associations or neighbourhoods, to support individual efforts to achieve self-sufficiency.[35]

Individuals seeking assistance under W-2 were offered four work options. The first was the primary objective and subsequent options were offered only as temporary expedients on the way to a normal job.

The first priority was unsubsidised employment, which was encouraged by job-placement help and advice about in-work benefits. As a second best, subsidised employment was provided. Employers could receive a monthly payment to offset the cost of training and supervision. The third best option was a community service job for those who needed to learn work habits. They were required to work 30 hours a week plus ten hours training. The fourth option was a programme for people genuinely unable to perform self-sustaining work, either through illness or incapacity. They were required to work 28 hours per week in a community rehabilitation programme or a volunteer activity, possibly with an additional 12 hours training.

No less important than encouraging self-sufficiency through work was the encouragement of intact families. Teenage parents were expected to complete their school education and required to live at home or in supervised hostels. There were no cash entitlements for unmarried teenage mothers and no cash benefits for any parent without the work obligation, unless their child was under 12 weeks of age.[36] Resident parents were required to co-operate in identifying the absent parent (in nearly all cases the father). In return, full child support payments went to the resident parents without any deductions.

The obligation of fathers to support their children was rigorously enforced. All non-resident parents were required by law to become more employable so that they could support their children. Failure to participate in work experience or training could lead to jail.[37]

The Wisconsin style of workfare has been criticised because compulsion was involved, as if there were an option that could involve no compulsion at all. The difficulty is that when individuals refuse to work because they are better off on benefits they are taking it for granted that other people will be compelled by the government to give some of their income to them. The only consistent stance for the person who wishes to avoid all compulsion is to call for no money to be given whatsoever. But if cash assistance is to be made available, then the real issue is how to give it without doing more harm than good. Wisconsin's intention was to restore independence, and it can be contrasted with the attitude of those who are content to pay benefits, whether out of sympathy or a pragmatic desire to keep the poor quiet. The relationship between claimants and the state can be seen as a contract. The contract between the state and individuals requires the state to maintain a national minimum and individuals to work if they are able.

Similar schemes were implemented throughout the USA and had a massive impact on welfare dependency. Between 1996 and 1999 the number on welfare fell by nearly half. Dependency had increased from 147,000 families (under one per cent of the American total) in 1936 to over five million families (about 15 per cent of the total) in 1994, with most of the increase in the late 1960s and 1970s. By June 1999 the number had fallen by half to around 2.5 million. Fifteen states experienced falls of over 60 per cent.[38] In March 2008 only 1.6 million families were claiming TANF and the number of individual recipients was 3.8 million.[39]

Implementation in the UK

Could such a scheme be implemented in Britain? My proposals fall into two groups.[40] First, we need to redefine the social contract between the community and its members. The safety net should always be there to prevent hardship, but we need to define clearly the work and other obligations that go with it. Second, we should abolish all entitlements to benefit and, instead, place an obligation on the government to provide temporary assistance sufficient to prevent severe hardship to all who ask, and to do so in a manner likely to lead to self-sufficiency.

Among those who accept the necessity for radical welfare reform are people who want to restore the national insurance basis of the social security system.[41] They believe it will avoid the necessity for a discretionary system of social assistance. During the course of the twentieth century it came to be accepted that people who needed help should be given it as of right and not as an act of kindness. Charity came to be associated with stigma and subservience. This distinction between 'benefits as an entitlement' and 'charitable assistance at the discretion of the donor' has its roots in the private welfare systems that pre-dated the welfare state. Before the watershed legislation, the 1911 National Insurance Act, it was common to make a distinction between charity and mutual aid. Those who had contributed to a friendly society thought of their benefits as a right, earned by their earlier contributions, and they prided themselves on never asking for charity. The 1911 scheme built on this distinction by extending the friendly society benefits to everyone in the national insurance scheme.

Friendly society members could genuinely claim to be entitled to their benefits, which were paid from a common fund accumulated from the small but regular contributions of members. However, from the very beginning national insurance had a 'something for nothing' element ('ninepence for fourpence', as Lloyd George put it). Thus, from the beginning, the full cost was not met by the members.

Campaigners for national insurance have typically wanted to reduce the need for discretion, but the 1911 Act failed to achieve it. The poor law[42] continued to offer discretionary benefits until 1948, only to be replaced by a similar discretionary system, national assistance, later renamed supplementary benefit and then income support.

We now find ourselves repeating mistakes made by an earlier generation. During the nineteenth and early twentieth centuries a distinction was not only made between charity and mutual aid, but also between two kinds of charity: the dole charities and the visiting charities. Like many government programmes in our own time, the dole charities associated kindness with 'refraining from judgement'. They gave cash without questions. The 'visiting' charities, however, tried to restore self-respect and independence and believed that to give cash without practical advice and encouragement to be independent was the easy but damaging option. British governments since the 1920s have often given benefits as a right and repeated the error of the old dole charities. During the Blair years the language of rights and responsibilities was intended to come to terms with this mistake, but it is only since the Freud report in 2007 that the necessary degree of personalisation has been seriously contemplated.[43] It remains to be seen whether the plan will be effectively implemented.

National insurance has its place but it is not possible to build a complete welfare system on it because most of the people today who are dependent on means-tested benefits have no national insurance entitlement and could not genuinely qualify in the near future. The challenge, therefore, is to devise a method of giving the kind of help that will restore genuine independence. If it is to be effective, such help must be discretionary because, apart from their reliance on benefits, claimants often have little else in common. The causes of their dependence are numerous and each requires a more personal service than the modern social security system has so far provided.

To summarise: the purpose of a discretionary welfare system should be to avoid pigeon-holing people and to take into account each individual's full circumstances with the intention of helping them to become self-sufficient. In most cases, complete self-support through work should be the aim, but for some, only partial self-sufficiency will be attainable. The distinction between contributory and non-contributory benefits should be abolished and a single income-replacement benefit introduced. It should be given a name such as 'transitional assistance' to emphasise that it is providing temporary support to help people back to independence. What would the work obligation mean in practice for two main groups: able-bodied people and single parents?

Reasonable work obligations: able-bodied people

New applicants should be subject to strict requirements before any benefit is paid. All should meet a personal adviser to determine their capacity for self-sufficiency. Where one parent is absent, the payment of child support by the absent parent should be investigated immediately. Once benefit has been paid the main aim should be to direct the claimant towards work.

Recipients of jobseeker's allowance (JSA) are already expected to make a genuine effort to find full-time work. However, they are not ultimately *required* to find work. The Government requires claimants to attend an interview, but except for the under-25s it is legitimate for them to turn up and announce that they have no intention of working.

Unsubsidised work should always be the first choice with other options only temporary until the ultimate objective of unsubsidised paid employment is met. Training should not be ranked as an equal alternative to work. Unfortunately Labour's original new deal for the 18-24 age-group treated training as one of four equal options, but it can too easily be used as a tactic to delay finding a job and the first priority should be to obtain paid work. In any event, work and training are not mutually exclusive alternatives. All work involves learning of some kind, formal or informal.

Reasonable work obligations: broken families

Quite apart from the emotional and educational impact on the children, it is very difficult for any parent simultaneously to work full-time and care for young children.[44] A highly-paid single parent may be able to afford to pay for childcare out of his or her wages, but the great majority of single parents cannot. Governments can adopt one of three general attitudes to households containing children: neutrality; privileging marriage; or privileging *non*-marriage. In recent years public policies have consistently privileged *non*-marriage.

The Obligations of Absent Parents: Public policies should put the interests of children first and bear in mind that in the vast majority of cases there are two living parents: one absent and the other resident. Most resident single parents are lone mothers and the first priority should be to ensure that the absent father is meeting the cost of raising his own children. In some cases, the amount that fathers can pay will allow the respective mothers to avoid work altogether, and in all cases it will enable them to be self-supporting with the addition of income from part-time work.[45]

Again, it is necessary to have available some sanctions against errant fathers. Such measures were taken for granted until recently. The 1948 National Assistance Act enabled the National Assistance Board (NAB) to trace and prosecute men who failed to maintain their dependants. In 1965 the board prosecuted 594 such men and 244 were sent to prison. The 1965 NAB annual report argued that prosecution was necessary 'not only to bring home to the man his liability to maintain his dependants but also to deter other would-be offenders'.[46] In 1967 there were 716 prosecutions of 'liable relatives' leading to 52 jail sentences. Every year until 1982 there were about 500-600 prosecutions and in that year there were 356 leading to 37 prison sentences.[47] However, criminal proceedings fell out of favour in the 1980s and in 1991 there were four prosecutions none of which resulted in prison sentences.[48] In 1993 the Child Support Agency (CSA) took over responsibility for child maintenance, although a husband and wife are still responsible for supporting each other. Criminal prosecution continues to be available to the DWP and should be used.

Since 2003 absent parents have been required to pay a percentage of their net income towards the upkeep of their child, 15 per cent of net income for one child, 20 per cent for two, and 25 per cent for three or more.[49] In February 2006 it was announced that the system would be radically overhauled. Subsequently the Child Maintenance and Other Payments Bill was introduced in Parliament in 2007. It proposes to replace the Child Support Agency with a new body, the Child Maintenance and Enforcement Commission. In October 2008 the bill was still under discussion.

One of the factors that undermined the CSA was its enforcement of the same formula on both divorced and unmarried men. In the early 1990s public opinion was strongly against unmarried men who fathered a child and refused to take any responsibility. But the CSA proceeded to direct its energy disproportionately against divorced men, some of whom were subject to existing court orders.

To avoid unfairness, all maintenance cases involving marriage breakdown should be dealt with by a judicial process leading to an independent judgement made after hearing both sides.[50] One of the defects of our current divorce law is that it tends to assume—it adopts as a legal fiction—that marriage breakdowns involve equal blame or an amicable parting or both. But in many cases one partner selfishly walks out on the other, imposing costs on the spouse and the distressed children. No-fault divorce enjoys considerable support, but we have not yet struck the right balance between, on the one hand, the interests of the children and, on the other, the interests of parents.

The Obligations of Resident Parents: Having required the father to pay the maximum support possible, the mothers should normally be required to work to the extent necessary to avoid welfare dependency. Widows and widowers with dependent children, however, should face no work obligation. But all other resident single parents who ask for welfare benefits should be subject to the same work requirement as other able-bodied persons.

The chief difficulty is deciding when the work obligation for the resident parent should be imposed. In Britain, in early 2008 there was no obligation other than to attend a work-focused interview until the youngest child is 16. Deciding at what age the work obligation should apply is a real conundrum. There is probably a consensus for a work obligation when the youngest child reaches school age, and such an obligation should be imposed at the earliest date thereafter. Since October 2008 lone parents have come under pressure to work when their youngest child is 12 and from 2010 when the youngest child is seven. Many people would argue that pre-school children are better off in the care of their mother than in childcare institutions, however well trained the staff might be. The evidence has long supported that view, especially for children up to the age of about three.[51] Marriage not only makes it possible for mothers to choose between work and childcare, it is also over-whelmingly in the interests of children. Studies comparing the average consequences of being brought up in different household situations show that when children are brought up by their two married parents they are the substantial beneficiaries. Probably no set of research findings in social science have produced such uniform results.[52]

Experience has shown that, if the government substitutes for the father, the results for the child are harmful; the mother experiences a lower income than if married; and the number of parents who opt for non-marriage increases. Consequently, an obligation to work is in the long-term interests of both mothers and children because it is likely to reduce the incidence of lone parenthood.

5. Scrap working tax credit and replace with a hard-work top-up

Earlier in this chapter I referred to people who are willing to work hard, but who are genuinely able to earn very little. The least defensible aspect of working tax credit is that benefit is paid to people who work as few as 16 hours a week. In effect, by working only part time, individuals can have their wages made up to the equivalent of a full-time income.

The guiding principle of reform should be that individuals are responsible for improving their income and for controlling their expenses. Moreover, what most people intuitively feel about welfare is *not* that no one should ever be poor, but rather that no one who has *worked hard* should be poor. How could such a principle be part of a welfare policy?

A minimum wage has a part to play, but if a person has made a reasonable effort to earn as much as possible and is still on an unacceptably low income, are further measures defensible? It is not possible for public officials to judge in detail whether a given individual or family has made a reasonable effort to increase earnings and control expenses, but it would be feasible to apply a simple test of whether a 'reasonable effort' had been made. Such rules are notoriously open to abuse but a requirement to work a minimum number of hours would be harder to mismanage or fake than most. The figure could be 35 hours a week for 47 weeks per year.[53] If working tax credit were abolished and replaced by a supplement payable only to claimants who had worked for 35 hours a week for 47 weeks a year, the benefit system would reward hard work instead of idleness. It would also assist couples who wanted to share work and childcare. The subsidy would be available for a single-earner family or if both parents worked part-time and shared child-care duties, and would serve far less as a public subsidy of family breakdown.

6. Income splitting for families

As B. Seebohm Rowntree pointed out, two main stages of the lifecycle put the family budget under strain. First, raising children adds to costs at a time when income may fall if one partner concentrates on childcare. And second, as age takes its toll, income may fall due to retirement from work and expenses may rise because of failing health.

Since 1925 British governments have used their powers of compulsion to require people to contribute towards a pension, and since 1948, when family allowance was introduced, the state has taken part of the responsibility for redirecting earnings towards families with children. In practice, it has assumed some responsibility for the two main periods of the lifecycle when expenditure is in danger of exceeding available resources.

Instead of transferring benefits to people when they have children, it would be preferable to allow parents to keep what they have earned. In some other countries couples are allowed to apportion their family earnings as they believe best. Draper and Beighton, in a study for CARE, have estimated that 45 per cent of the population of OECD countries they studied benefit from income-splitting regimes or similar systems.[54]

In France, for example, the '*quotient familial*' allows people to split their income between parents and their children. An adult counts as one unit and a child half a unit so that a married couple with two children would be able to divide their income between three units and a childless couple between two.

How might income splitting work in the UK? In September 2008 the UK personal allowance was £6,035. For a couple with two children and a single breadwinner earning £30,000, income splitting on the French formula would allow the total to be divided into three units of £10,000. If each unit benefited from a tax allowance of £6,035, the family would have significantly more income, which could be used to divide work and child care in different ways.

With one earner and a total income of £30,000 income tax of 20 per cent (£4,793) would be paid on £23,965. If there were three units, tax would be payable on £11,895 at 20 per cent (£2,379). Imagine that the man works 30 hours a week, cares for the children one day a week, and earns £20,000, while his wife earns £10,000 and cares for the children for four days. Their tax liability would be the same whether the husband worked full-time and the wife was a full-time carer, or if they reversed roles completely. Under the current system in the UK, the wife's personal allowance would be unused if she had no earnings.

Another variation would be to allow income to be assigned to any related adult living at the same address. Families who took responsibility for caring for their elderly parents, for example, could assign their income to them and pay less tax to reflect the saving to other taxpayers. Grandparents could undertake child care duties, thus releasing parents to work. Such flexibility would obviate the need to regulate the workplace by imposing maternity leave on employers who can sometimes ill afford it. Employers could focus on what they are good at and leave couples to arrange their own affairs. It might even add to productivity by eliminating regulatory costs.

7. Old age: require provision for the state minimum only

Is it realistic to expect people to take personal responsibility for self-support during old age? It is widely accepted that the presence of a safety net may encourage some individuals to rely on the state rather than their own endeavours. This difficulty is at the heart of the current debate about pension reform. To what extent should provision of a pension be compulsory?

At present national insurance contributions are compulsory and entitle paid-up contributors to receive the basic pension. Payment towards the state second pension (also called the Additional State Pension, abbreviated as S2P and previously known as SERPS from 1978-2002) is also compulsory, although individuals can 'contract out' and pay their national insurance contributions into a private pension. Despite being contributory, both the basic pension and S2P are pay-as-you-go systems, financed from current tax revenues and not from a separate actuarially-sound fund.

In 2008/09 the Basic State Pension (BSP), a pension by right based on NI contributions, was £90.70 per week for a single person and £145.05 for a couple. At present a man will receive a full BSP after making contributions (or being treated as if he had made contributions) for 44 of the 49 years between ages 16 and 65. People without a full contribution record receive a partial pension. The state pension is payable at age 65 for men and 60 for women, but between 2010 and 2020 it will become 65 for both.

However, someone who has not paid sufficient contributions to earn the full pension simply has their income topped up under the Pension Credit scheme, previously called the Minimum Income Guarantee (MIG). There are two elements: the Guarantee Credit and the Savings Credit. In 2008/09 the Guarantee Credit topped income up to £124.05 per week for a single person aged 60 or over. For example, someone with £100 pre-benefit income (including BSP, SERPS, S2P and any private pension) would have received an additional £24.05 in guarantee credit.

At age 65 Savings Credit may apply. A single person with an income above £124.05 or a couple with an income above £189.35 could be eligible. In 2008/09 the maximum Savings Credit was £19.71 per week for a single person and £26.13 for a couple.

One feature of this complex system is that many people do not claim what they are entitled to. Some people are too proud, and others are too confused, to apply. The DWP estimated that during the financial year 2004/05 between 61 and 69 per cent of those eligible claimed pension credit.[55]

Additional benefits are also payable. Housing Benefit is a means-tested benefit paid to people living in rented accommodation and pensioners who receive the Guarantee Credit automatically receive Housing Benefit. Housing Benefit is normally withdrawn at the rate of 65p for each additional pound of income above the threshold. But in order to prevent pensioners from having their Pension Credit payments removed through the Housing Benefit taper, it is not reduced until income reaches the level of the Guarantee Credit plus the maximum Savings Credit.

Council Tax Benefit (CTB) is a means-tested benefit that assists people with Council Tax and entitlement is calculated according to the same formula as Housing Benefit. The taper rate for CTB is a 20p reduction for each pound in excess of the threshold. As Housing Benefit and CTB are calculated together, the combined deduction from benefits, when someone is entitled to both, is 85p for each pound of extra income.

Disability Living Allowance (DLA) is a tax-free, non-contributory and non-income-related benefit to cover the extra costs of people who are severely disabled before reaching the state pension age. It is not possible for someone aged 65 or over to make a new DLA claim, but people who claim and qualify for the allowance before reaching age 65 can keep it after that age, so long as they continue to satisfy the conditions.

For people who are aged 65 and over when they claim help with disability-related extra costs, Attendance Allowance (AA) provides a tax-free, non-contributory and non-income-related benefit. DLA and AA are not taken into account in calculating entitlement to Pension Credit, Housing Benefit or CTB, but they entitle recipients to disability premiums for Housing Benefit and CTB and to receive the disability additional amount under Pension Credit.

In addition pensioners are eligible for a variety of other cash and non-cash benefits, including the Winter Fuel Payment which was £250 in 2008/09 for a household with someone aged 60 or over or £400 if aged 80 and over. A free TV licence is available for those who live in a household where someone is aged 75 and over and prescriptions and eye tests for those aged 60 and over are also free.

The Pensions Commission estimated the cost of these additional benefits for 2004/05. The total cost of the Winter Fuel Payment and the free TV licence was £2.9 billion plus a further £7 billion for Housing Benefit and Council Tax Benefit. Expenditure on AA and DLA was put at £6.5 billion in 2004/05.

For many, being a pensioner has become a story of claiming extras from the state. Reforms due to be introduced from 2012, according to the government white paper of May 2006, do not radically alter the situation. Individuals will be required to contribute four per cent of their income between bands of earnings of roughly £5,000 and £33,000 and employers will make contributions of three per cent, although employees can opt out.[56]

Many would prefer a system that offered hope of an adequate income without the necessity for means testing.

Four main alternatives to pay-as-you-go systems are generally put forward. The first requires payment of compulsory contributions but allows individuals a choice of pension provider. This is the system in Chile. It is defended as increasing choice compared with a scheme requiring a compulsory contribution to a state pension. The second approach is a funded state pension. The third alternative is free market provision but with tax breaks to encourage people to lock their savings into private pension schemes. The main line of reasoning used in support of this method is that people are short-sighted and, without the encouragement of tax concessions, will not choose the most suitable means of saving.

The fourth approach prefers to put few, if any, limits on the methods by which people can provide for their old age and also, as far as possible, avoids using the tax system to encourage particular types of provision. The government in this view should neither discriminate between methods of provision, nor require contributions to any given scheme. But, the government retains the responsibility for providing an income safety net for those who fail to provide for themselves.

Public policies should have two basic aims. First to reduce compulsion to the minimum necessary to prevent imposition on other people and otherwise to leave people free to make their own arrangements, either as individuals or as families committed to each other across the generations. Second, to get as close as possible to tax neutrality between various types of investment. It is not easy to accomplish without having unforeseeable rebound effects on the economy, but major distortions should be removed.

The temptation to rely on state benefits instead of making adequate contributions earlier in life is the result of offering unconditional benefit payments on reaching a certain age.

The Government has accepted that this system creates a moral hazard, but it has chosen to deal with it by coercing people who do not need to be coerced, many of whom have made arrangements more suitable for their own circumstances than any pension, whether a basic state pension or the state second pension.

A more effective method of reducing the moral hazard would be to require individuals to build up a fund sufficient to buy an annuity equivalent to the state minimum. One such scheme was proposed some years ago by New Zealand's Sir Roger Douglas. Under his scheme, once a sufficient fund had been accumulated, saving would be voluntary.[57] On retirement individuals would have to buy the minimum annuity required by law. Any balance could be taken as a lump sum, used to buy an additional annuity, or left to accumulate further interest.[58]

8. Raise the retirement age to 70

We should also raise the state retirement age. Not everyone wishes to 'retire'. Some people want to lead a 'useful life' until they die or become incapable of work. Most people retiring at 60 or 65 nowadays are capable of working for many more years. In May 2006 the Government announced that it intended to increase the retirement age to 67 by 2044, but the state pension age should be raised more rapidly in stages, perhaps by six months per year so that in ten years it will be 70.

9. Create family trust funds for lifecycle saving

The current tax regime for pensions should be revised. At present payments into a personal pension are subject to tax relief at each person's marginal rate: 20 per cent for basic rate taxpayers in 2008/09 and 40 per cent for higher rate payers. One approach would be to replace current tax arrangements with the tax regime for Individual Savings Accounts (ISAs), but with much higher investment limits. People could invest in savings instruments with after-tax income and no tax would be payable on the growth of the fund or on income earned from the investment. Such funds might be called family trust funds. No tax would be payable on withdrawal or closure. If any balance remained on death, there should be no inheritance tax. Such a system would provide something close to tax neutrality for all methods of saving from after-tax income. Schemes could evolve with the minimum of regulation offering any combination of saving methods. They could be combined with insurance or be invested for income or capital growth. There could be long-term lock-in or short-term access, or they could be linked or not linked to annuities. To avoid a sudden impact on the economy it might be necessary to limit the amount that can be paid in during a tax year—perhaps to the whole of a person's annual income.

What strategies could an individual pursue in this environment? First, there is 'work till you drop'. A prudent person could plan to go on working until he or she was no longer able to do so. In some cases such a person would die while still working, and in others he or she would work until illness or frailty intervened.

It would also be perfectly prudent for a family to follow a cross-generation plan. A family could build up assets— property, jewellery or other durable goods—as well as shares or cash savings in a family trust fund with the intention of handing their assets on from generation to generation. Purchasing an annuity involves giving a capital sum to an insurance company which undertakes to pay an agreed sum per year until death. The insurer takes the risk that the capital will run out, but members of a family might prefer to take that risk themselves through the family trust fund.

Such a property-based strategy would be suitable for families of quite modest means. For most people, investing in the family home has been a good long-term bet for the last 100 years or so, and by trading up or down, or using the property as collateral for a loan, cash can be made available at different stages of the lifecycle. Scrapping inheritance tax would further encourage mutual support across the generations.

To sum up: pension provision would be a personal responsibility, but no one would be allowed to fall below the state minimum. Everyone should be expected to save enough to avoid relying on the work of other people in their old age, but any compulsion should be kept to a minimum.

Conclusion

Such would be the principles consistent with a 'membership state' in which everyone was expected to do their bit to be independent, with the absolute assurance that no one will fall below the national minimum if things go wrong. Such a guarantee, if it is to endure, can only be based on a system of reciprocal obligation.

4

Independence and Schools

In its annual report for 2006/07 Ofsted ranked 10 per cent of secondary schools as 'inadequate'. It rated 13 per cent of secondary schools as 'outstanding', 38 per cent as 'good', and 39 per cent as 'satisfactory'.[1] The Government has also failed some of its own targets. For example, it aimed to ensure that at least 85 per cent of 11-year-olds achieved level 4 or above in key stage tests. In 2006/07 only 80 per cent met the standard in English and only 77 per cent in maths.[2] The Government has also failed its own standard of ensuring that 85 per cent of 14-year-olds achieve level 5 or above in English, maths and ICT, and 80 per cent in science. In 2006/07 level 5 was achieved by 74 per cent in English; 76 per cent in maths; 74 per cent in ICT; and 73 per cent in science.[3] The Government just scraped past its target of ensuring that 60 per cent of those aged 16 achieve the equivalent of five GCSE's at grades A*-C. In 2006/07 60.3 per cent achieved the standard.[4] However, critics have shown standards have fallen, partly by increasing the proportion of children who take subjects that are easier to pass. The Government denies this claim but tacitly accepted its validity when from 2006 it published figures showing how many children got five A*-Cs including English and maths.

International comparisons confirm the doubts about standards. Results from the OECD's Programme for International Student Assessment (PISA), released in 2008, provide conclusive evidence that whilst government exam scores have been rising, standards have in fact fallen. Between 2000 and 2006 there was a 28 point decline for reading amongst UK 15-year-olds: a decline from 23 points above the OECD average, to only three points above

79

average. This is a drop from 7th to 17th place in PISA's international rankings. In maths there was a 34 point decline amongst UK 15-year-olds: a decline from 29 points above average, to three points below average. This is a drop from 8th to 24th place in PISA's international rankings. Government results show rising standards at all expected levels between 2000 and 2006. In English an eight percentage point rise at Key Stage 3 (14 years old) is claimed and a seven percentage point rise at GCSE. In maths a 12 percentage point rise at Key Stage 3 (14 years old) is claimed and nine percentage point rise at GCSE. Another international study, Progress in International Reading Literacy Study (PIRLS) revealed a similar trend. It found that England dropped from 3rd place to 19th place between 2001 and 2006.

On average our schools do not compare well with those in other developed countries. However, the overall rankings conceal an important truth, namely that while our best schools are probably as good as the best schools elsewhere, we have a disproportionate number of under-performing schools that let down their pupils, especially those from poorer backgrounds.

My argument is that we will only be able to overcome this problem if we restore to the majority of parents the independence they have earned by working for a living. Only then will parents have the power to uphold the high standards their children need to flourish in modern societies. Some countries, notably Germany, appear to have made a success of centralisation, but whatever the reasons for German success, centralisation in Britain over many decades has not worked.

Private action for the public good

I will compare two rival approaches based on contrasting interpretations of the main mechanism of change or improvement: (1) exclusive and concentrated state power for the public good and (2) private action for the public good.

Exclusive and concentrated state action assumes that the best approach is to discover the 'one best solution' and impose it through agencies that have powers of compulsion—it is 'rolled out' nationally from Whitehall. The government organises and directs schools, sets targets, and even stipulates the hours that must be devoted to particular subjects.

Private action for a public purpose is based on the view that the primary engine of improvement is pluralistic experimentation, free inquiry into the best methods of teaching, and mutual learning through open discussion of successes and failures. It encourages social entrepreneurship and supply-side liberalisation. An improving system is a voyage of discovery that never quite ends.

The two approaches differ in the role allocated to parents. Champions of state monopoly look upon parents from the perspective of the system. They often seem to be thinking of two schools with equally motivated and able teachers, one serving a rich area and one a low-income area. The school in the poor area can't overcome the disadvantages of having unsupportive parents—which seems unfair to them.

The schools' results are assumed to reflect the home environment and the solution is to spread around the beneficial influence of the wealthy parents—perhaps through lotteries as in Brighton, or banding by exam attainment as in Bradford to ensure proportionate representation of the main ability groups, or by re-drawing school catchment area boundaries to mix up the social classes. At the same time, however, the people who want the beneficial influence of wealthy parents to be more widely distributed are inclined to insult the same parents as 'middle class', or 'pushy' middle-class parents.

How does that approach compare with private action for the common good? The dispute is not about the facts of the current situation. Most children go to neighbourhood schools. People tend to congregate in areas based on the housing they can afford, their social class and their race. It frequently turns out that the schools in wealthy areas tend to be better than those in poorer areas. Critics who argue that choice only benefits the rich have this type of situation in mind. If popular schools in well-off neighbourhoods are full, then school choice leads to waiting lists or selection.

But the remedy is not to spread middle-class parents across all schools, it is to allow new schools to be easily established. Can it be done? Who will benefit? What can we learn from other countries? Some have evolved different public/private combinations that provide more effectively for children from low-income backgrounds.

Before looking at what we can learn from overseas experience, it is important to be clear about the aims of a good school and in particular to remind ourselves that education is not just about examination results.

The aims of a good school

In a nation viewed as a membership association, what should be the role of the government in education? The primary responsibility for education should lie with parents, but the government on behalf of the whole society should provide a reliable helping hand when necessary. Moreover, education has a special significance in a free society. The task of each generation of adults is to pass on to their children the values and knowledge necessary to preserve our liberal-democratic way of life. Much of this work takes place in the family, but schools are also central. Their task is not only to turn out youngsters trained to fill a narrowly economic role, but also to play their part in equipping young people with the habits and skills they will need to be full participants in a society of freely co-operating individuals.[5]

Most parents expect a school to teach their children the basics, including handling numbers, spelling correctly, reading fluently and writing clearly. Schools have also traditionally taught children about the history of their own civilization and tried to pass on its strengths, as well as pointing out its defects. In recent decades, however, many schools have fallen prey to cultural relativism so that teaching the virtues of British culture was seen as improperly 'taking sides', where they have not adopted a perverse one-sided hostility to all accounts of past British achievements. Many schools have also failed to play their part in upholding the moral consensus on which any free community depends. Some schools even fail to keep order on their own premises, as a recent report by Ofsted testifies. In March 2005 the Chief Inspector of Schools reported that about 20 per cent of schools had claimed that 'gang behaviour' was widespread.[6]

We urgently need a public debate about the purposes of education. A good place to start would be the era before schools became the plaything of politics. The ethos of government schools in Britain at the beginning of the twentieth century is well described in the 'Introduction to the Elementary Code' of 1904:

> The purpose of the Public Elementary School is to form and strengthen the character and to develop the intelligence of the children entrusted to it, and to make the best use of the school years available, in assisting both girls and boys, according to their different needs, to fit themselves, practically as well as intellectually, for the work of life.

> And, though their opportunities are but brief, the teachers can yet do much to lay the foundations of conduct. They can endeavour, by example and influence, aided by the sense of discipline, which should pervade the School, to implant in the children habits of

industry, self-control, and courageous perseverance in the face of difficulties; they can teach them to reverence what is noble, to be ready for self-sacrifice, and to strive their utmost after purity and truth; they can foster a strong respect for duty, and that consideration and respect for others which must be the foundation of unselfishness and the true basis of all good manners; while the corporate life of the School, especially in the playground, should develop that instinct for fair-play and for loyalty to one another which is the germ of a wider sense of honour in later life.

In all these endeavours the School should enlist, as far as possible, the interest and co-operation of the parents and the home in an united effort to enable the children not merely to reach their full development as individuals, but also to become upright and useful members of the community in which they live, and worthy sons and daughters of the country to which they belong.[7]

The aim of policy should be to encourage more schools of the type described by this code. To that end a debate about abolishing the national curriculum is long overdue. It is not only too prescriptive but also associated with a faulty testing regime that has not accurately measured attainment. So long as the rigour of external examinations is maintained, each school should be permitted to devise its own curriculum.

The chief reason given for government involvement since 1870 has always been that education was of such central importance that no one should go without it. Hence, it was legitimate for the government to fill gaps in the availability of schools and ensure that no children were excluded because their parents were poor. In practice, however, state provision has for many years failed the least fortunate members of society. The worst performing schools are concentrated in localities where poverty is most prevalent and all but the most prejudiced observers would find it difficult to resist drawing the conclusion that state education has failed, not in some minor details, but to achieve its primary aim.

Moreover, it has failed because of the inherent flaws in the political process, namely over-concentration of power, the side-effects of political struggle including the manipulation of official information for party advantage, and the suppression of social entrepreneurs. We must search, therefore, for a new balance between government and citizens that confines central authority to what it can do best, without presuming to run everything. Before turning to specific proposals, we should first consider what we can learn from overseas and, in particular, we should ask if there is any experience that teaches us that a less politicised, unforced and pluralistic system can serve the interests of the poor more effectively than a state monopoly. Serving the interests of children from the poorest backgrounds is the crucial moral test that any policy must pass.

Learning from Overseas Experience

It has frequently been argued that monopoly is the cause of low standards in education and that a more competitive system would produce higher standards. A variety of approaches have been tried in different countries. The aim has been to create a market in education services similar to the private sector but with the government assuming responsibility for ensuring that all parents have the necessary purchasing power. In this model, the role of the government is no longer to provide education but to ensure that there is a functioning market and that everyone has access to what is on offer. The essential feature is that there should be no monopoly, public or private. It should be easy to establish a school, existing popular schools should be able to expand when necessary, and customers should be able to choose their preferred school. Some critics of state education accept the need for reform but advocate giving parents a choice between state schools. However, experience has shown that, if money does not follow the parents' choice, if popular schools cannot take on extra pupils, and new schools cannot easily be established, few advantages accrue.[8]

Pseudo-choice or effective choice

Voucher schemes have commonly been advocated as a more effective way of creating choice. Some have been implemented, but the evidence so far is that the exact characteristics of specific schemes make a major difference to the outcomes. The early version of Wisconsin's voucher scheme, for example, created few incentives for state schools to improve, as I show below. We can therefore distinguish between schemes based on pseudo-choice and those based on effective choice. Under the latter, parents have real purchasing power and there is supply-side freedom to expand and enter the market.

The modern debate about school choice has developed furthest in America, although other countries have played a part, not least Sweden. Since the 1970s US reformers have been pointing out that America was performing badly on international comparisons and that over the years attainments in University admission tests had been falling.[9] State schools in America are the responsibility of states, not the federal government, and are usually run by local school districts. The great majority are neighbourhood schools attended by all children in a given locality, and thus have an effective local monopoly. The two most significant anti-monopoly reforms have been voucher schemes, which allow parents to send their children to private schools, and the creation of a new type of semi-independent public school, the charter school, to compete with traditional public-sector schools.

The political left in the US has typically opposed school choice, claiming that it would serve the interests of the rich and not the poor. They have frequently been hostile to private schools and charter schools and demanded equality in the form of obliging all children to go to government schools. They have often been accused of hypocrisy because the intellectual left tend to be among the better paid members of society and can afford to live in neighbourhoods with good schools. Suppressing competition does not affect their own children, who go to schools already performing to the satisfaction of parents. Some states have gone to great lengths to encourage racial mixing, often by busing children between segregated localities, but, despite these measures, throughout America there have continuously been prosperous neighbourhoods with good schools that well-off parents could buy their way into. As a result ostensibly egalitarian left-leaning intellectuals have been able to send their own children to good schools in these neighbourhoods because they could afford the higher house prices, while simultaneously preventing standards from being raised in poor localities through increased competition.

A good education system should provide opportunities for children from all backgrounds. But what is the best solution to the problem that children who go to schools achieving relatively lower standards are disproportionately from disadvantaged backgrounds? What kind of policy would avoid repeating or reinforcing the existing pattern of disadvantage without entrenching public-sector monopoly? Many experiments have been attempted and a furious battle is being fought between academics who appraise the schemes so far attempted. It is well established that charter schools in the US cater disproportionately for children from black, Hispanic and poor backgrounds and so few reputable academics have tried to claim that they are inequitable. Instead, opponents of competition typically try to produce studies showing that charter schools have not raised standards. Before turning to this evidence, what have been the main choice-based reforms?

Education vouchers

Vouchers can be either *universal,* applying to all children, or *targeted* at specific groups, usually the poor or those attending failing schools.

Universal Vouchers: Sweden

Sweden is the only European country operating a universal voucher scheme. The reforms began in 1992 when independent schools were guaranteed the right to receive funding from municipalities.[10] Vouchers were valued at 85 per cent of the average cost of a place in a local state school. In 1995 the figure was reduced to 75 per cent before being increased to 100 per cent in 1997.[11] Today, any type of school, whether religious, for-profit or charitable, that meets the requirements of the National Agency for Education (NAE) is entitled to this funding. Schools are prohibited from charging top-up fees and are not allowed to select pupils by ability. They must also meet specific academic standards and adhere to the Swedish national curriculum.[12]

The voucher system has resulted in an increase in independent providers. Before the reforms, independent schools in Sweden accounted for less than one per cent of pupils and few of those received any government funding.[13] Most schools were run by municipal authorities. In the first ten years of the voucher programme, the number of independent schools rose from 90 to 475.[14] According to the Swedish National Agency for Education there were 585 independent schools in 2005, accounting for nearly 12 per cent of compulsory schools.[15]

An independent study found that competition from independent schools has improved results in state schools. Moreover, it has been found that new independent schools are more likely to be established in areas of under-performing state schools serving disadvantaged children.[16]

Targeted vouchers

There are two types of targeted voucher. One is means-tested, and aimed at enabling children from poor families to attend a better school. The other is targeted at giving pupils who attend failing schools the opportunity to attend a better school, irrespective of their income.

Income target: Milwaukee

In 1990, the city of Milwaukee in Wisconsin established the Milwaukee Parental Choice Program (MPCP), a system of means-tested vouchers to give real choice to low-income families by paying for them to attend registered independent schools. Parents with an income at or below 175 per cent of the poverty line could claim a voucher initially worth $2,500. However, until the scheme was reformed in 1998 it had only a minor impact. At first the number of participating pupils was capped at one per cent of total Milwaukee pupils, well below the number who qualified. Despite an increase to 1.5 per cent in 1993 the number of Milwaukee schools facing effective competition was very small. Public schools also suffered no income loss and the voucher was worth only 38 per cent of the public school cost per pupil. It is generally accepted that, until the scheme was revised in 1998, vouchers created very little competitive pressure. However, from that year the value of the voucher was doubled to about $5,000 and around 50 per cent of the funding came from the Milwaukee Public Schools budget. The ceiling on enrolment was increased to 15 per cent of Milwaukee pupils, which meant that from 1998/99 elementary schools in Milwaukee faced substantial competition.

Research by Caroline Hoxby of Harvard University into the effects of targeted vouchers in Milwaukee found that students taking part in these programmes performed better in tests than a control group of otherwise similar students. She was able to compare three types of school: those most subject to competition had two-thirds or more of pupils eligible for vouchers (32 schools); those subject to some competition with less than two-thirds of their pupils eligible (66 schools); and a control group of other Wisconsin schools outside Milwaukee that were urban and had at least 25 per cent of pupils on free or reduced-price lunches and whose pupil populations were at least 15 per cent black (12 schools).

For reading, pupils were classified as attaining a 'minimal', 'basic' or 'proficient or advanced' standard, and each child's score was then ranked from one to 100. After improved vouchers were introduced in 1998/99, the proportion of 4th grade pupils (aged 9-10) in the schools subject to most competition attaining the highest standard was up four national percentile rank points and for those classified as having 'minimal' reading ability the proportion fell nine national percentile rank points.

In maths at 4th grade, the effect of the voucher programme on the schools most subject to competition after between two and four years was an increase of eight national percentile rank points. In science there was an increase of 13 rank points. The performance of the control group remained flat.[17] Compared with the monopoly era before 1998, competition raised standards for everyone, and the bigger the risk of losing pupils to rival schools the greater the improvement.

In January 2005, 13,978 pupils were using vouchers to attend 117 independent schools.[18] Moreover, there was good evidence to suggest that the targeted voucher programmes were reaching the pupils they were designed for. 175 per cent of the poverty line was $32,532 for a family of four in 2003/04.[19] In Milwaukee, the average income of families taking part in the programme was $10,860 in 2000, with 76 per cent of students coming from lone-parent households. Hoxby's research is supported by studies conducted by Jay P. Greene of the Manhattan Institute. He found that standardised test scores for pupils using vouchers for three or more years in independent schools were on average higher than for a control group of state school pupils.[20] In later research he also found that Milwaukee pupils using vouchers to attend independent schools graduated at a higher rate than those in state schools: 64 per cent compared with 36 per cent.[21]

Failure target: Florida

Since 1999, Florida has been operating a targeted voucher programme known as the Florida A+ Plan for Education. This programme provides pupils who attend failing state schools, defined as those receiving an 'F' grade from the Florida Department of Education twice in a four-year period, with 'Opportunity Scholarships' to attend independent schools (including religious schools) or a more successful state school. School grades are based on pupil performance in the Florida Comprehensive Assessment Tests (FCATs) in maths, reading and writing, as well as on attendance, discipline and dropout rates. In 2004/05, 690 pupils used the vouchers to attend 34 schools and the average value of a voucher was $4,241.[22] Research by Jay P. Greene into the Florida A+ Plan found that 'Florida's low-performing schools are improving in direct proportion to the challenge

91

they face from voucher competition.' The study further concludes that state schools facing most voucher competition showed the *most* improvement.[23]

The supply side

The Netherlands and the USA offer the two most prominent examples of supply-side liberalisation that has made it far easier for independent organisations to establish and run schools. In England, the final decision over school places rests not with parents, but with local education authorities (LEAs). The majority of parents, who cannot afford to opt-out of the state system, are lumbered with the schools in their locality.

Free schools in the Netherlands

Freedom of supply has been enshrined in the Dutch constitution since 1917. Any group of parents or other interested party has the right to set up an independent school. Just 50 parents are required to establish a school in municipalities with fewer than 25,000 inhabitants and only 125 parents in areas with more than 100,000.

The ease of entry for independent providers means that around 70 per cent of Dutch children attend independent schools.[24] It has also encouraged diversity. Among secondary schools, 32 per cent are state schools, 34 per cent Catholic, 27 per cent Protestant and seven per cent do not fit any of these categories.[25] Moreover, due to the increased number of providers, the average size of schools is relatively small: an average elementary school has only 160 pupils.[26]

Funding is based on a per-pupil system. Once parents have decided to send their child to a school, the full amount is paid directly from the Ministry of Education to that school. This system is not a voucher arrangement, where parents are given a cheque to spend at a school of their choice. Although the money follows the pupil in the same way, it is invisible to the parents. It does mean, as with a voucher system, that the power of parents to exit is strong and if a school is unpopular it could be forced to close or change its approach.

The amount paid for each child in primary schools is weighted according to socio-economic background. Those from poor backgrounds can receive up to 190 per cent of the standard funding.[27] Although it is easy to open a school in the Netherlands, once in existence, schools receiving state funding are subject to strict regulations: all schools must teach the national curriculum, face regular inspections and take national exams. Additionally, the progress of every child is tracked and so, while this system has opened up supply, it has done little to ease the regulatory burden faced by schools.

Charter schools in the USA

During the 1990s many states in the USA also began to liberalise the supply of education with the introduction of charter schools. The idea is that a public authority, normally the state board of education or the local school district, grants a charter (or contract) to a group of parents, a charity or a business to provide a school. Charter schools do not charge tuition fees, and are non-religious and non-selective. The school board finances the school on a per-pupil basis, which means that, as in the Netherlands, if the school does not attract enough pupils, it may have to close. In September 2006 there were over 3,900 charter schools serving over one million pupils in 40 states.[28]

Again, like the Netherlands, the intention of the reform was to encourage independent providers. Unlike in the Netherlands, however, another intention was to reduce central regulation of such schools, in order to free social entrepreneurs from the bureaucracy facing state schools. Although the degree of such freedom varies greatly between states, generally charter schools enjoy a worthwhile degree of independence from political control. They cannot select their students based on admissions tests, and must obey many public school regulations, including test requirements, but they are often exempt or partially exempt from regulations about teacher certification. To avoid back-door selection, state laws typically require charter schools to select students by lottery when the number of applicants exceeds the number of available places.

Battle has raged over whether charter schools have raised standards and whether they are equitable, that is, have they served the interests of the already well off more than those of disadvantaged pupils? A US Department of Education study in 2004 has often been quoted as evidence that charter schools are ineffective. It looked at charter schools in five states in 2001/02 and found that they were less likely to meet state performance standards. But the study was based on a snapshot and did not look at improvement over time. Moreover, the report itself warned that 'it is not possible to determine from this study whether or not traditional public schools are more effective than charter schools'.[29]

The US Department of Education published another report in August 2006. It claimed that pupils in traditional public schools scored 4.2 percentile points more than pupils in charter schools in reading and 4.7 percentile points more in maths, after adjusting for demographic characteristics such as gender, race, poverty, home resources and 'limited English proficiency'. The study was based on the findings from the 2003 National Assessment of Educational Progress (NAEP), a national sample survey of attainment often called the nation's report card.

Christopher and Sarah Lubienski looked separately at maths results from the 2003 NAEP. The sample of 4th graders (aged 9-10) was made up of 126 charter schools and 6,104 public schools.[30] Charter schools scored 4.4 percentile points lower than traditional public schools in the 4th grade after adjustments using hierarchical linear modelling, one of the many statistical programmes the purpose of which is to compare two otherwise similar groups, only one of which is subject to the influence being studied. The authors concluded that: 'Overall, this study suggests that charter schools are neither the unqualified failure that detractors claim, nor that there is something inherent in the independent structure of charter school organisation that promotes greater student achievement, as choice enthusiasts would have us believe.'[31] However, it also concedes that:

> national NAEP data tell us little about local differences among schools. For instance, it is becoming increasingly difficult to speak of 'charter schools' because of the great variation between the authorizing legislation in different states. A wide variety of charter schools has emerged—some small-scale independent operations, others run by management companies, some with a particular social mission, others with a for-profit orientation. The present analysis treats charter schools as monolithic when they are not.[32]

The Department of Education and the Lubienski studies relied on the NAEP, which as we have seen is a sample survey that includes only a few charter schools. The first comprehensive study of all elementary charter school pupils (aged 5-11) was carried out by Caroline Hoxby from Harvard University. It studied pupils in the 4th grade (aged 9-10) in 2002/03, some 50,000 pupils.[33] Charter schools were compared to public schools that pupils would otherwise have attended, defined as the nearest public school with a similar racial breakdown. The proportion of pupils judged proficient in the nearest state school was compared with the proportion judged proficient in each charter school, and the difference calculated. These results were then averaged for all charter schools and for all state schools in the study, and the result expressed as the percentage difference between the scores of all charter schools and all state schools in the study. Charter schools were 5.2 per cent more likely to be proficient in reading and 3.2 per cent more likely in maths, according to state examination results and after deducting charter schools that catered for 'at-risk' or gifted pupils. (Many charter schools have been established specifically to cater for disadvantaged pupils.) The performance gap increased with the length of time a charter school had been operating: in reading it was an additional 2.5 per cent for schools that had been operating between one and four years; 5.2 per cent for schools 5-8 years old; and 10.1 per cent for those in operation for 9-11 years.[34]

Charter schools were less likely to have white pupils and far more likely to have black and Hispanic pupils, as well as poor pupils. Hoxby concluded that charter schools '…are disproportionately drawing students who have suffered from discrimination… in the public schools'.[35]

So far we have looked at studies based on the NAEP sample survey and a study of every charter pupil in the 4th grade. Both rely on making statistical adjustments to single out the impact of charter schools as such, as distinct from the effect of socio-economic characteristics such as income or race. The most reliable method of identifying the impact of charter schools is the randomised control trial, but such experiments are not easily established. However, Caroline Hoxby and a colleague from Columbia Business School looked at three charter schools in Chicago in 2001/02, where school places were allocated by lottery when a school was over-subscribed. The study compared the achievements of pupils selected by lottery to attend the Chicago International

Charter School with those who were not (and who, consequently, mainly attended local state schools). This method has the advantage of eliminating the selection effect that statisticians worry about. The results cannot be explained by 'home background' because all the pupils had motivated parents who wanted their children to attend charter schools—some were lucky enough to win the lottery to attend and others were not.[36]

Maths results are reported as percentile scores. Whether or not the results were adjusted for influences such as gender, ethnicity, participation in the federal free or subsidised lunch programme and their need for special education, maths results for charter school pupils were six to seven percentile points higher and for reading five to six points higher.[37] The students were mainly black or Hispanic. Most received free or subsidised lunches, which means that they fell below 185 per cent of the federal poverty line.

Charter schools were especially likely to raise the achievement of pupils who were poor or Hispanic. In mainly Hispanic areas the advantage was 7.6 per cent in reading and 4.1 per cent in maths, whereas in a typical charter school the advantage was 4.2 per cent in reading and 2.1 per cent in maths. In high-poverty areas the advantage was 6.5 per cent in reading, compared with 2.6 per cent for other charter schools.

Egalitarians think that school diversity and competition will benefit only children who already do well, and further handicap those not doing well, but these results show that it is the least advantaged who gain the most. A pluralistic system that drives up standards by permitting energetic new entrants to shake up the existing schools tends to benefit the poorest people most.

So far I have taken studies of attainment in charter schools compared with other public schools in America at face value. But they suffer from a serious flaw, quite apart from any methodological criticisms of sample surveys and the usefulness of statistical techniques for taking into account influences such as race or income. The studies assume that anyone claiming that charter schools are effective must show that they achieve better academic results than nearby public schools, whereas the chief defence of competition is that, by ending monopoly, it will raise standards in all schools subject to competitive comparison with rivals. It is not easy to devise a study that demonstrates such an effect, but we should not fall into the trap of accepting that charter schools should only be judged successful if their pupils achieve better results than those in other schools. Competition has the potential to lift standards in all schools, private and state, as the Wisconsin study revealed.

The Way Forward

As Chapter 2 described, there are degrees of state control. Five points along a continuum from independence to subjugation can be distinguished: private voluntary payment; compulsory private payment to avoid imposition; taxation followed by partial return as earmarked spending power; taxation and provision through competing institutions; and taxation and provision through government monopolies.

The NHS is at the most controlled end of the continuum and our schools are similar. Formally there is some choice of school, but in practice it is limited. My argument is that the majority have earned the right to independence by supporting themselves through work. If we allowed people to pay less tax and spend their earnings on services everyone would benefit. Moreover, it will encourage competition, which is in the common good.

The family remains the best institution for raising children, and schooling works best when parents are closely involved. An effective public policy should aim to limit the government to tasks within its competence and to restore everything else to civil society. There are three main aims: first, ensure that all parents have the spending power to determine their children's education; second, transfer state schools to the independent sector to end public sector monopoly; and third, de-regulate the supply side to encourage the founding of new schools.

Spending power

Restoring the responsibility for education to parents matters because it encourages the family and the school to work in partnership. This is only really possible if schools rely on parents for their income, which is achievable in a variety of ways. Ideally it would be accomplished though direct parental payments, though for many this is out of the question. It can also be achieved with a voucher system — allocating parents a voucher sufficient in value to buy education in a school of their choice. Or parents could be empowered through the tax system. For example, if all parents were free to buy education as each thought best, they would have a right to deduct up to an agreed amount (let's say £6,000) from their tax liability. People whose tax liability exceeded £6,000 would pay less income tax and people whose tax liability was below £6,000 would receive an income tax credit.

Vouchers

Critics of state monopoly in schooling have traditionally argued for a voucher scheme, under which parents receive a certificate sufficient in value to buy education in a school of their choice. Schools that attract parental support will flourish; and others will find it necessary to mend their ways or close. Some authors add to the basic idea an element of equalisation: children from low-income families, for instance, would be given vouchers with a higher cash value to make up for the poverty of their home background.[38]

The chief risk of a voucher scheme is that governments will abuse their power to define which schools are entitled to receive public funds. Such power could be used so restrictively that an effective public-sector monopoly would be maintained. One possible answer is to lay down only minimal conditions, covering relatively few matters such as health and safety and minimum standards for teacher certification, so that the registration of schools under the scheme could not become a significant barrier to the entry of new schools. Teachers, for instance, should not be required to undergo lengthy training. A bachelor's degree or its equivalent for secondary schools might be sufficient (as it once was), and for primary teaching a demonstrated sense of vocation should be adequate.

A second approach would be to bar the government from laying down conditions for the acceptance of voucher finance, and to leave full responsibility to parents. For instance, a rule might be enforced giving a school able to attract a minimum number of pupils (perhaps 50) a right to receive voucher finance. A cross between the two approaches might be better still. For instance, the government could maintain a register of schools that meet defined requirements, and a register of those that do not. Vouchers would be payable to registered and unregistered schools, thus leaving it to parents to decide whether they valued registration as an indication of merit or not. Private schools should, of course, be included.

A particular problem with public-sector regulators is that they tend to err on the side of caution and proceed by imposing procedural checks that are supposed to eliminate unwanted risks, such as paedophiles working in schools. The impact of such checks often proves to be disruptive without significantly reducing the danger.[39] However, the Swedish National Agency For Education could have blocked the growth of independent schools in Sweden but in fact encouraged them. The English Schools Commissioner, established in 2006, has a formal duty to encourage school diversity but in its current form the officeholder can achieve little. The role could easily be extended to encourage the foundation of new schools. If the criterion of success were the extent of competition, the regulator could be an ally.

Ten years ago state funding of more or less any school chosen by parents could have been contemplated with equanimity, but today a new concern has emerged, namely the danger that schools will teach sectarianism, hatred or even encourage terrorism. This publication is not the place to go into this complex question, but one thing should be clear. It is a legitimate role for the government to maintain personal security and eliminate crime, and if it needs to inspect schools to ensure that a particular religion is not teaching animosity towards other faiths or encouraging violence, it should do so with all necessary vigour.

Far from meting out only a bare minimum for the poor, a voucher scheme would enable low-income parents, in combination with sympathetic teachers and activists, to offer their own answers to the problems of low-quality schools. It would only require a few people of good will to transform radically the life-chances of low-income families. No longer would it be necessary to convince local officials and politicians of the merits of one's case. It would be enough to

101

convince only the relatively few parents and teachers necessary to establish a school.

A voucher system could work like this. The government would supply parents with a voucher (literally a piece of paper that can be presented to a school in place of cash) worth the cost of educating one child for one year, currently about £6,000 on average. Needless to say, the value of the voucher would have to vary according to the age of the child.

Should topping-up be permitted? Egalitarians object strongly to any scheme that allows parents to add to the value of the voucher, and some advocate giving a voucher of higher than normal value to children from low-income backgrounds. The chief argument against topping up is that well-off parents will buy places in schools that can afford smaller classes and better equipment, thus reinforcing the existing pattern of inequality. First of all, parents can and do send their children to such schools now. The wealthiest private schools do achieve high standards for their pupils, although the reasons have a good deal to do with the ethos of the school rather than expenditure per head. Beyond a certain point spending per pupil makes little difference to attainment. To be in a class of 40 may be a disadvantage, but many teachers accept that once the class size is reduced to about twenty the advantages of further reductions are much diminished. There is an optimum class size and the value of the voucher should be set to permit a school to achieve it. If the voucher were priced so that no class size needed to be more than 20 (a common maximum in the private sector), every child would have access to schools able to provide education in reasonable class sizes. One of the striking features of US charter schools, however, is that they receive less funding per pupil than nearby state schools, despite having a disproportionate number of children from disadvantaged backgrounds. (US private schools also tend to cost less per pupil than US public schools.) The key to the relative success of charter schools evidently does not rest primarily on expenditure per head, but rather on effective management.

In any event it is quite simply wrong to penalise parents who want the best for their children. The state as a membership association should never suppress the potential achievements of any individual, nor condone jealousy. If some parents wish to spend more than others on their children's education they should be permitted to do so, whether they are spending out of their excess income or scrimping and saving to give their children the best they can afford. It is surely highly anomalous that objections are rarely raised to parents spending freely on frivolous self-indulgences, while spending freely on their child's education is the subject of constant rebuke. The primary obligation of the nation as a membership association is to ensure that every child has access to a good education, not to discriminate against well-paid parents.

Apart from being morally wrong it is in practice beyond the capabilities of government to prevent wealthy parents from benefiting their own children. A government can, however, make sure that the funding received by schools never falls below a level sufficient to provide a good standard (such as class sizes of 20).

The prevailing attitude to parents who want the best for their children is a prime example of the Government's failure to respect people who are vital to the success of any society. A parent who provides a supportive home is likely to be denounced as a 'pushy' parent or merely described with a bit of a sneer as 'middle class'—condemnation enough for some hard-core equalisers. Invariably the parents who are condemned as middle class or pushy have done no more than to provide supportive homes and to try to find the best school available locally. Any morally justifiable reform should harness and build upon the energy and commitment of such parents. Declaring war on them is folly for everyone.

So long as it is easy to establish new schools their efforts to seek out the best for their children will benefit everyone, as studies of Wisconsin, US charter schools and Sweden have demonstrated. It is only when the power of the state is used to restrict school places that competition becomes a zero-sum game.

An education tax allowance

A second approach would be to allow every eligible family an annual amount sufficient to pay for education but to transfer it through the tax system. At present we all pay taxes and receive education as a benefit in kind. But we do not know the amount we personally pay in taxes for schooling and we do not know the cost of any one state school. We therefore do not know whether we are net contributors to the public purse or net beneficiaries. We also have no reason to seek better value for money.

The Office For National Statistics prepares annual calculations based on tenths of the population, already mentioned in Chapter 3, but the major difficulty is that none of us are able to work out whether or not we are net contributors. Only about a quarter of General Government Expenditure is met by income tax. Indirect taxes (such as VAT and duties on alcohol and petrol) are about 60 per cent of government revenues and are paid by all sections of society. What would a tax credit of £6,000 mean for a family in the middle of the income distribution?

If we were all given a school tax allowance of £6,000, based on ONS estimates, the 7th decile (between the 60 per cent and

70 per cent marks) of non-retired households with children paid, on average in 2006/07, £5,904 in income tax. The 6th decile paid £4,575 and the 5th £3,415—all less than the value of the voucher. The top three deciles paid more than £6,000 in income tax. However the 7th decile also paid indirect taxes of £6,512, the 6th paid £5,658 and the 5th, £5,915. Overall, every decile from the 4th upwards would be a net contributor if indirect taxes were taken into account. The majority of us, therefore, have earned the right to independence.

Transferring state schools to civil society

It is doubtful whether demand-side changes will alone be sufficient to break the power of entrenched public sector monopolies in the UK. Schools should have total control of admissions, school numbers, governing structure, teacher tenure, training and salaries. Ideally they should set their own fees and not be accountable for their performance to any political authority, but only to parents. It is very difficult to see how such independence could be accomplished without radical supply-side de-regulation. Moreover, the teachers' unions are one of the biggest obstacles to the improvement of education standards and their power results from the centralised nature of education management. Decentralise management power, and you also decentralise union power, which is why the unions have typically resisted any such change.

It is now well established that the key to the successful functioning of any market is the possibility that new entrants will attract customers from existing providers. For this reason, it would be desirable for neither central government nor local authorities to have the power to run any new schools, and to relinquish control of existing schools. This could be accomplished by means of a phased hand-over to independent educational trusts. Primary schools in particular could be run by people in each locality, thereby providing a way of harnessing the energy and commitment of public-spirited people everywhere. As Mill pointed out, when the state monopolises everything it drives out opportunities for public service and self-development.

The Government's white paper of October 2005 was presented as a scheme for increasing diversity of schooling and parental choice. The changes were more than cosmetic, but they were a compromise between factions who wanted very different things, as the bitter disputes over the education bill in 2006 revealed. Egalitarians particularly disliked the correlation between the social and economic background of parents and the scholastic achievements of children, and the summary of the white paper reflected this dislike when it said that educational achievements were still 'too strongly linked to their parents' social and economic background—a key barrier to social mobility'.[40] Another group was worried about the workforce failing to remain competitive with overseas rivals in a 'knowledge-based economy' and a third group believed in choice and diversity. The Education and Inspections Act of 2006 was a compromise between them, compounded by a further division, that between local authorities who wanted to preserve their power and a central government that hoped to ensure country-wide compliance with its policies. The advocates of higher standards saw the local authorities as part of the problem, obstructing improvements and especially the expansion of popular schools or building new ones. As the white paper conceded, expansion meant getting permission from all the main rivals who were represented on the school organisation committee that existed in every local authority. These committees have been abolished, but the local authorities continue to control school planning: 'Local authorities will need to plan how many schools their local area needs, where and how big they need to be, what kind of schools will serve the area best, and who the schools should serve.'[41] The prevailing attitude of local authorities is revealed by the remarks made by one local education authority official who frankly stated when speaking to the House of Commons Select Committee on Education: 'We are not in the business of moving children out of schools to go to more popular schools. We are generally not in the business of expanding schools to meet demand.'[42]

Moreover, the new 'trust' schools remain 'part of the local authority family of schools'. The national curriculum continues to apply, along with the assessment regime and national agreements about teachers' pay.[43] The power of the centre has been increased by creating a new Schools Commissioner who will have the power to push local authorities in the direction wanted by central government.

Supply-side de-regulation

There should no longer be a public sector monopoly, and new schools should be able to emerge without needing prior permission from the authorities. Freedom of entry would be especially advantageous in areas of concentrated poverty because it would permit teachers with a special sense of mission to assist the poor by founding new schools. As argued earlier, competitive markets are voyages of discovery. We should not assume that parents' current preferences are their final view. Those who have carefully considered their decision can change their view in the light of experience. Many will not have thought about it very much. Others will not feel well informed when they make their choice of school. The main driver of success is always supply-side innovation. New departures are typically the result of groups of teachers or philanthropists, or enthusiasts for a particular religion resolving to run a school in a particular way. The parents as consumers always have the final say, but they will be able to make better choices if innovators and social entrepreneurs are free to take the lead.

Opposition party reform plans

The Conservative manifesto at the 2005 General Election advocated a scheme that closely resembled the Swedish system. Parents were to have a 'right to choose' any school in the state system. Local councils would no longer allocate places. Parents would also be able to send their child to any independent school that would provide 'good education' for the average costs of a place in the state system, about £5,500. No additional fees could be charged.

The Conservatives realised that new school places would be necessary to create genuine choice and planned to fund an additional 60,000 places over five years. There would be a 'right to supply' by providers, including faith groups, charities, parents and private companies. The plans were abandoned when David Cameron became leader, but in the Conservative party green paper of 2008 the same idea re-emerged in a diluted form.

They latest plan is to de-regulate the supply side so that new state schools can be established by philanthropists, parents groups and others. The 'new academies', as they are to be called, will receive state funding and enjoy a degree of freedom from central direction. The Tory green paper says that the scheme resembles the Swedish system more than any other but there is one big difference. The Swedish government funds genuinely independent schools. The new academies are to be state schools accountable direct to the Secretary of State. The Opposition has understood that to make a reality of parental choice new places are needed. It also acknowledges that autonomy is important, but it has not taken on board the importance of independent ownership and management of schools as a safeguard against state interference.[44]

In Sweden the Government made no provision for the capital cost. The rapid growth of independent schools in Sweden since 1992 was financed privately, often by commercial developers. Nevertheless the Conservatives are planning to use public funds to build the new academies. The Brown Government has allocated £9.3 billion under the Building Schools for the Future programme and the Conservatives intend to re-allocate 15 per cent of it to their new academies. Over nine years the grand total available would be £4.5 billion, which at £20,000 per place would allow over 220,000 new school places to be provided.

But if the Conservatives win in 2010, will this money still be there given the current state of our public finances? If not the programme could founder and that is why it is important to learn from Sweden's experience. No start-up costs were available from the Government and according to the Swedish Association of Independent Schools, a majority of their members rent property in the market. Often, developers renovated office buildings and converted them into classrooms. They put up the capital investment because they had the guarantee of an income stream from the Swedish Government. The secure income stream was enough.

But, it's not only that the capital may not be available in 2010, the necessity to apply for capital grants from a government agency is a potential choke-point that could be manipulated by hostile officials intending to undermine the scheme from within. Land in the UK is more scarce than in Sweden, and perhaps capital grants may be needed in some urban areas, but if there is to be a supply side revolution the more we rely on private initiative the better and the faster we will be able to raise standards for the large minority of children who attend failing state schools.

Exclusions

Normally a school would expect to be able to remove pupils who were seriously disruptive. However in a competitive system it can seem as if disruptive pupils are being irresponsibly foisted onto other schools. In Sweden, for example, to avoid this danger it is almost impossible to expel a pupil. It would be best if UK schools continued to take responsibility for pupils who proved to be disruptive unless they have committed serious crimes against the school, its teachers or pupils. Disruptive pupils, however, cannot be allowed to remain in normal classrooms and each school could provide its own unit for unruly pupils either on their own site or in partnership with nearby schools.

Conclusions

Education works best when parents play their part in co-operation with the school, but if they do not, then schools must compensate for parental neglect. The vital change we need today is to end public-sector monopoly to open the way for inventive newcomers. The mistake we made during the twentieth century was to believe that the state was the best agency for discharging the common good. We have now learnt that it might not be. Indeed, our problem today is that the schools in the poorest areas are among the worst, which means that the state has failed to discharge its main responsibility, namely to prevent early disadvantage acting as a break on achievement throughout adulthood. The reality is that the power of the state, initially conceded to fill gaps in private provision and to fulfil shared public goals, has been captured by groups with other purposes. Education became an instrument of social engineering during the twentieth century led, especially in the 1960s and later, by politicians who resented the grammar schools that since 1902 had been such an important channel of upward social mobility for academically-able working-class children. Today state education is dominated by producer-oriented local authorities and teacher unions.

Any proposal on how this problem of capture by producer interests might be solved must demonstrate how the ideal of ensuring education for all could be better accomplished in the independent sector than in the sphere of state control. Historically education for disadvantaged children was made available privately. It could be again. The challenge today is to provide practical examples of reforms that demonstrably work in their educational interests.

To summarise: public policy for education should have three main aims. First, it should guarantee access for all to a high minimum standard of education. The government should ensure that all children are educated (though not necessarily in school) and ensure that parents' income is not a barrier to a good standard of education. A voucher scheme would be a step in the right direction but a tax allowance would be better still. Second, all schools should be independent of political control, including over-intrusive Ofsted inspections. To that end the government should transfer the ownership of state schools to non-profit trusts. Third, the government should de-regulate the supply side to encourage the founding of new schools.

Notes

1: Introduction

1   Marshall, P. and Laws, D. (eds), *The Orange Book: Reclaiming Liberalism*, London: Profile Books, 2004.

2   Cohen, N., *What's Left: How Liberals Lost Their Way*, London: Fourth Estate, 2007; Anthony, A., *The Fallout: How a Guilty Liberal Lost His Innocence*, London: Jonathan Cape, 2007.

3   Collins, P. and Reeves, R., 'Liberalise or die', *Prospect*, June 2008.

4   Norman, J. and Ganesh, J., *Compassionate Conservatism*, London: Policy Exchange, 2006.

5   Kruger, D., *On Fraternity*, London: Civitas, 2007.

6   Carswell, D. and Hannan, D., *The Plan*, London: Lulu, 2008.

7   Jenkins, S., *Thatcher and Sons*, London: Allen lane, 2006.

2: The Guiding Principles of a Free People

1   Locke, J., *Second Treatise of Government*.

2   Holmes, S., *The Anatomy of Antiliberalism*, Harvard: Harvard University Press, 1996.

3   Smith, A., *The Theory of Moral Sentiments*, Indianapolis: Liberty Fund, 1976, p. 167.

4   *Theory of Moral Sentiments*, p. 269.

5   Blackstone, *Commentaries on the Laws of England*, London: University of Chicago Press, 1979, vol. 3 , p. 4.

6   Locke, J., *Second Treatise of Government*, s.13.

7   Smith, A., *Theory of Moral Sentiments*, Indianapolis: Liberty Fund, 1976.

8   Montesquieu, *Spirit of the Laws*, Cambridge: Cambridge University Press, 1989, p. 155.

9   Locke, J., *Second Treatise of Government*, s. 6.

10 Kant, I., *Political Writings*, Cambridge: Cambridge University Press, 1991, p. 46.

11 Kant, *Political Writings*, p. 42.

12 Kant, *Political Writings*, p. 45.

13 Kant, *Political Writings*, p. 44.

14 Milton, J., *Areopagitica and Other Political Writings*, Indianapolis: Liberty Fund, 1999.

15 'Power tends to corrupt; absolute power corrupts absolutely' – Lord Acton, Letter to Mandell Creighton.

16 Locke, J., *Conduct of the Understanding*, Indianapolis: Hackett, 1996, p. 169.

17 Locke, J., *Some Thoughts Concerning Education*, Cambridge: Hackett Publishing, 1996, pp. 140-41.

18 Locke, *Conduct of the Understanding*, Indianapolis: Hackett, 1996, p. 186.

19 Locke, J., *Four Letters on Toleration*, London: Alexander Murray, 1870 (reprint of 7th edn).

20 Smith, A., *Wealth of Nations*, Indianapolis: Liberty Fund, 1976.

21 Mill, J.S., *Principles of Political Economy*, London: Longmans, 1909, p. 947.

22 Bevan, G. and Hood, C., 'Have targets improved performance in the English NHS?', *BMJ* 2006;332;419-422.

23 Popper, K., *Open Society and Its Enemies*, London: Routledge & Kegan Paul, 1945, vol 1, chapter 9.

24 Mill, J.S., *Principles of Political Economy*, London: Longmans, 1909.

25 Smith, A., *Wealth of Nations*, Indianapolis: Liberty Fund, 1976, vol II, pp. 687-88.

26 Mill, J.S., *On Liberty*, Cambridge: Cambridge University Press, 1989, p. 109.

27 *On Liberty*, p. 115.

28 *On Liberty*, p. 110.

29 *On Liberty*, p. 110.

30 *On Liberty*, pp. 111-12.

31 *On Liberty*, p. 113.

32 Green, T.H., 'Lecture on liberal legislation and freedom of contract' in Nettleship, R. (ed), *Works of Thomas Hill Green*, London: Longmans, 1906, p. 372.

33 Green, T.H., *Lectures on the Principles of Political Obligation*, London: Longmans, 1948, p. 225.

34 *Lectures on the Principles of Political Obligation*, 225.

35 *Lectures on the Principles of Political Obligation*, p. 226.

36 Green, T.H., 'Lecture on liberal legislation and freedom of contract', p. 375.

37 Hobhouse, L.T., *Liberalism*, London: OUP, 1964, p. 91.

38 Berlin, I., 'Two concepts of liberty', in *Four Essays on Liberty*, Oxford: Oxford University Press, 1969.

39 Polanyi, M., *The Logic of Liberty*, Indianapolis: Liberty Fund, 1998.

40 Green, D.G., *Working Class Patients and the Medical Establishment*, London: Temple Smith, 1985.

41 Locke, J., *Second Treatise of Government*, Cambridge: Cambridge University Press, 1988, s. 133.

42 Locke, *Second Treatise of Government*, s. 22.

43 Goodhart, David., *Progressive Nationalism: Citizenship and the Left*, London: Demos, 2006.

44 Hayek, F., *The Constitution of Liberty*, London: Routledge, 1960, pp. 221-25.

45 Hart, H.L.A., *Punishment and Responsibility*, Oxford: Clarendon Press, 1968; *The Concept of Law*, Oxford: Clarendon Press, 1961.

3: Independence and Welfare

1 DWP, *Five Year Strategy* 2005.

2 *Client Group Analysis*: Quarterly Bulletin on the Population of Working Age on Key Benefits, August 2003, Department for Work and Pensions; HMRC, Child and Working Tax Credits Statistics, April 2006.

3 DWP Tabulation Tool. Working Age Client Group Caseload; HMRC, CTC and WTC Statistics, April 2008.

4 DWP, Tax Benefit Model Tables 2008.

5 Brewer, M., Proportion of households, and individuals living in households, who have private incomes exceeding their net income from the state, London: Civitas, November 2008.

6 Bryson, A., Ford, R., and White, M., *Making Work Pay: Lone Mothers, Employment and Well-Being*, York: Joseph Rowntree Foundation, 1997, p. 39.

7 Millar, J., Webb, S. and Kemp, M., *Combining Work and Welfare*, York: Joseph Rowntree Foundation, 1997, p. 31.

8 Marsh and McKay, *Families, Work and Benefits*, London: Policy Studies Institute, 1993, p. 186.

9 Marsh, A., Lowering barriers to work in Britain', *Social Policy Journal of New Zealand*, Issue 8, March 1997, p. 126.

10 IFS press release: http://www.ifs.org.uk/pr/lone_parents_credits.pdf

11 IFS Green Budget 2007, p. 225.

12 http://www.ifs.org.uk/bns/bn70.pdf

13 DWP, Destination of benefit leavers, 2004.

14 Draper, D. and Beighton, L., *Taxation of Married Families*, London: CARE, 2008, p. 8.

15 Draper and Beighton, pp. 23-24.

16 Stewart, K., 'Towards an equal start?' in Hills, J. and Stewart, K. (eds), *A More Equal Society*, Bristol: Policy Press, 2005.

17 http://www.guardian.co.uk/commentisfree/2006/aug/11/comment.politics

18 Borjas, G., *Heaven's Door*, Princeton: Princeton University Press, 1999, p. 83.

19 Web: http://www.ucl.ac.uk/media/library/immigration

20 *Family Resources Survey 2006/07*, Department for Work and Pensions, Table 3.10.

21 *Family Resources Survey 2006/07*, Table 3.9.

22 Office for National Statistics, *Work and Worklessness Among Households*, August 2008, First Release.

23 DWP, *Abstract of Statistics for Benefits, National Insurance Contributions and Indices of Prices and Earnings 2005*.

24 Less the cost of public service occupational pensions, personal social services and administration costs.

25 HM Treasury, *Public Expenditure Statistical Analysis 2008*.

26 *Households Below Average Incomes 2006/07*, Table 4.12ts.

27 Novak, M. *et al.*, *The New Consensus on Family and Welfare*, Washington: AEI, 1987.

28 This is an updated version of arguments first put forward in my now out-of-print book, *Community Without Politics*, London, 1996.

29 Jones, F., 'The effects of taxes and benefits on household income, 2006/07', *Economic & Labour Market Review*, vol 2 no 7, July 2008, London: ONS, p. 37.

30 Jones, F., 'The effects of taxes and benefits on household income, 2006/07', *Economic & Labour Market Review*, vol 2 no 7, July 2008, London: ONS, Table 24.

31 Jones, F., 'The effects of taxes and benefits on household income, 2006/07', *Economic & Labour Market Review*, vol 2 no 7, July 2008, London: ONS, Table 23.

32 Green, D.G., *Reinventing Civil Society*, London: Civitas, 1993.

33 See *Reinventing Civil Society*.

34 Rogers, J., 'Designing work-focused welfare replacement programmes', *Social Policy Journal of New Zealand*, Issue 8, March 1997, p. 68.

35 Rogers, *SPJNZ*, p. 73; Turner, J., 'Radical changes to the welfare system in the US state of Wisconsin: the results', in Turner, J. *et al.*, Europe's Welfare Burden, London: Civitas, 2002.

36 Rogers, *SPJNZ*, p. 75.

37 Rogers, *SPJNZ*, pp. 71,76; Mead, L., *From Welfare to Work: Lessons From America*, London: IEA, 1997; Mead, L. (ed.), *The New Paternalism: Supervisory Approaches to Poverty*, Washington, DC: Brookings Institution, 1997.

38 Besharov, D. and Germanis, P., *Ending Dependency*, London: Civitas, 2001, p. 62.

39 US Department of Health and Human Services, Administration for Children and Families; http://www.acf.hhs.gov/programs/ofa/data-reports/caseload/caseload_current.htm

40 Based on proposals first published in Green, D.G., *An End to Welfare Rights*, London: Civitas, 1999.

41 For example Field, F., *Stakeholder Welfare*, London: IEA, 1996.

42 The responsibilities of the poor law unions were transferred to local authorities in 1930 but the poor law was not fully abolished until the enactment of the 1948 National Assistance Act.

43 http://www.dwp.gov.uk/publications/dwp/2007/welfarereview.pdf

44 The results for the US are summarised in McLanahan, S. and Sandefur, G., *Growing Up With a Single Parent: What Hurts, What Helps*, Cambridge, Mass: Harvard University Press, 1994.

45 Marsh, A., 'Lowering the barriers to work in Britain', *Social Policy Journal of New Zealand*, Issue 8, March 1997, p. 131.

46 Quoted in George, *Social Security*, 1968, pp. 230-31.

47 DHSS, *Social Security Statistics 1982*, p. 219.

48 *Social Security Statistics 1992*, p. 39.

49 Web: www.csa.gov.uk

50 For an excellent discussion of marriage as a contract see Barry, N. in Whelan, R. (ed.), *Just A Piece of Paper? Divorce Reform and the Undermining of Marriage*, London: IEA, 1995.

51 Morgan, P., *Who Needs Parents?: The Effects of Childcare and Early Education on Children in Britain and the USA*, London: IEA, 1996.

52 McLanahan and Sandefur, *Growing Up With a Single Parent*, 1994. Dennis, N., *Families Without Fatherhood*, (3rd edn) London: Civitas, 2000.

53 From October 2007 statutory holiday entitlement was increased to 24 days including 4 bank holidays. From April 2009 it will be 28 days including bank holidays.

54 Draper and Beighton, *Taxation of Married Families*, 2008, pp. 16-17.

55 ONS, *Pension Credit Estimates of Take-Up in 2004/2005*.

56 *Security in retirement: towards a new pensions system*, DWP, May 2006, Cm 6841.

57 Douglas, R., *Unfinished Business*, Auckland: Random House, 1993, pp. 152-53.

58 Douglas, *Unfinished Business*, pp. 164-65.

4: Independence and Schools

1 The Annual Report of Her Majesty's Chief Inspector of Education, Children's Services and Skills 2006/07. Ofsted 2007, HC1002, p. 25.

2 DCSF, *Autumn Performance Report 2007*, Cm 7279, p. 26. The provisional 2008 results were available, but the final numbers were not available at the time of publication.

3 DCSF, *Autumn Performance Report 2007*, Cm 7279, p. 31.

4 DCSF, *Autumn Performance Report 2007*, Cm 7279, p. 39.

5   Based on Green, D.G., *From Welfare State to Civil Society*, Wellington: New Zealand Business Roundtable, 1996.

6   *Guardian*, 1 March 2005.

7   Introduction to the New Code of the Public Elementary School, 1904, in Maclure, J.S. (ed.), *Educational Documents: England Wales 1816-1968*, London: Methuen, 1969, pp. 154-55.

8   Hoxby, C.M., *School Choice and School Competition: Evidence from the United States*, Swedish Economic Policy Review 10, 2003, pp. 24-28; http://post.economics.harvard.edu/faculty/hoxby/papers/hoxby_2.pdf.

9   The SAT was at one time an acronym for the scholastic aptitude test that was administered by the College Board (and carried out by the Educational Testing Service, a non-profit organisation) on behalf of universities and colleges to provide a standard measure of achievement on which to base college admissions. From 1994 it was announced that SAT was no longer an acronym. It provided a stable benchmark for much of the post-war period but the test was recalibrated in 1995 and again in 2005.

10 Bergstrom, F. and Sandstrom, M., *School Choice Works! The Case of Sweden*. Issues in Thought, vol 1, issue 1, Friedman Foundation, 2002, p. 4.; http://www.friedmanfoundation.org/schoolchoiceworks/swedenstudy0103.pdf.

11 Pollard, S., *A Class Act: World lessons for UK education*. Adam Smith Institute, 2001, p. 15; http://www.adamsmith.org/policy/publications/pdf-files/a-class-act.pdf.

12 Hockley, T. and Nieto, D., *Hands Up for School Choice! Lessons from school voucher schemes at home and abroad*. Policy Exchange, 2004, p. 11; http://www.policyexchange.org.uk/uploads/media/school_choice.pdf

13 Bergstrom and Sandstrom, *School Choice Works!* 2002, p. 3.

14 Hockley and Nieto, *Hands Up for School Choice!*, 2004, p. 12.

15 Cowen, N., *Swedish Lessons*, London: Civitas, 2008, p. 14.

16 Sandstrom, F. and Bergstrom, F., *School Vouchers in Practice: Competition Won't Hurt You!* The Research Institute of Industrial Economics, Working Paper No. 578, Stockholm, Sweden, 2002, p. 23; http://www.iui.se/. See also, Cowen, *Swedish Lessons*, 2008.

17 Hoxby, *School Choice and School Competition: Evidence from the United States*. Swedish Economic Policy Review 10, 2003, p. 29-31; http://post.economics.harvard.edu/faculty/hoxby/papers/hoxby_2.pdf.

18 http://www.dpi.state.wi.us/dpi/dfm/sms/doc/mpc04fnf.doc

19 *The ABCs of School Choice*, Friedman Foundation, 2004-2005 Edition, p. 38; http://www.friedmanfoundation.org/ABC.pdf

20 Greene, Jay.P., and Peterson, P.E., Du, J. with Boeger, L., and Frazier, C., *The Effectiveness of School Choice in Milwaukee: A secondary analysis of data from the program's evaluation*, Program in Education Policy and Governance, Occasional Paper: 96-3, Harvard University, 1996. And: Greene, Jay P., Peterson, P.E. and Du, J. *Effectiveness of School Choice: The Milwaukee Experiment*, Education and Urban Society, 31 (2) Feb 1999; http://www.heartland.org/pdf/21844y.pdf

21 Greene, Jay. P., *Graduation Rates for Choice and Public School Students in Milwaukee*. School Choice Wisconsin, 2004. http://schoolchoicewi.org/data/currdev_links/grad_rate.pdf

22 *The ABCs of School Choice*, p. 14.

23 Greene, Jay P. and Winters, M., *When Schools Compete: The Effects of Vouchers on Florida Public School Achievement*, Education Working Paper, No. 2, Manhattan Institute for Policy Research, 2003; http://www.manhattan-institute.org/html/ewp_02.htm

24 Justesen, M., *Learning from Europe: The Dutch and Danish School Systems*, Adam Smith Institute, 2002, p. 17. http://www.adamsmith.org/policy/publications/pdf-files/learning-from-europe.pdf

25 Tooley, J., Dixon, P. and Stanfield, J., *Delivering Better Education: Market solutions for education improvement*, Adam Smith Institute,

2003, p. 15; http://www.adamsmith.org/policy/publications/pdf-files/delivering-better-edu.pdf

26 Hockley and Nieto, *Hands Up for School Choice!*, 2004, p. 15.

27 Hockley and Nieto, *Hands Up for School Choice!*, 2004, p. 14.

28 The Center for Education Reform; http://www.edreform.com/index.cfm?fuseAction=stateStats&pSectionID=15&cSectionID=44

29 US Department of Education, Evaluation of the Public Charter Schools Program, Final Report, 2004, DOC # 2004-08, p. xiv.

30 Lubienski, C. and Lubienski, S.T., Charter, Private, Public Schools and Academic Achievement: New Evidence from NAEP Mathematics Data, January 2006, p. 47; http://www.ncspe.org/publications_files/OP111.pdf

31 Lubienski, 2006, p. 36.

32 Lubienski, 2006, p. 38.

33 If 4th grade results were not available, 5th grade or 3rd grade results were used.

34 Hoxby, C., Achievement In Charter Schools And Regular Public Schools In The United States: Understanding The Differences, December 2004; http://post.economics.harvard.edu/faculty/hoxby/papers/hoxbycharter_dec.pdf

35 Hoxby, C., 2003, p. 59.

36 The Impact of Charter Schools on Student Achievement, Caroline M. Hoxby and Jonah E. Rockoff, November 2004. http://post.economics.harvard.edu/faculty/hoxby/papers/hoxbyrockoff.pdf

37 Hoxby and Rockoff, 2004, Tables 6a and 6b.

38 Le, Grand, J. and Estrin, S., *Market Socialism*, Oxford: Clarendon Press, 1989.

39 Furedi, F., *Licensed to Hug*, London: Civitas, 2008.

121

40 *Higher Standards, Better Schools For All*, DfES, 2005, p. 7.

41 DfES, 2005, p. 106.

42 *Right to Choose*, Conservative Party, p. 37;
    http://www.conservatives.com/pdf/rightochoose_education.pdf
    *Department for Education and Skills: Five Year Strategy for Children and
    Learners*, 2004, p. 50;
    http://www.dfes.gov.uk/publications/5yearstrategy/docs/DfES5Yea
    rstrategy.pdf

43 DfES, 2005, p. 28.

44 Conservative Party, *Raising the Bar, Closing the Gap*, Policy Green
    Paper, 2008.